LIST OF OFFICIALS

CIVIL, MILITARY, AND ECCLESIASTICAL

OF

CONNECTICUT COLONY

FROM MARCH 1636 THROUGH 11 OCTOBER 1677

AND OF

NEW HAVEN COLONY

THROUGHOUT ITS SEPARATE EXISTENCE

ALSO

SOLDIERS IN THE PEQUOT WAR

WHO THEN OR SUBSEQUENTLY RESIDED WITHIN
THE PRESENT BOUNDS OF CONNECTICUT

COMPILED BY

DONALD LINES JACOBUS, M.A.

CONNECTICUT TERCENTENARY PUBLICATION
OF THE CONNECTICUT SOCIETY OF THE ORDER OF
THE FOUNDERS AND PATRIOTS OF AMERICA

CLEARFIELD

Originally published by
The Connecticut Society of the Order of the
Founders and Patriots of America
New Haven, Connecticut 1935

Reprinted for
Clearfield Company, Inc. by
Genealogical Publishing Co., Inc.
Baltimore, Maryland
1989, 1996, 2000

International Standard Book Number: 0-8063-4641-8

INTRODUCTION

ALL persons holding office, civil or military, by colonial authority, in Connecticut and New Haven Colonies from March 1636 through October 11, 1677, are alphabetically listed in the following pages. Non-commissioned military officers are also included when their rank was conferred by colonial authority. To increase the utility of the List, ministers of parishes have been added, and the names of Pequot War soldiers so far as they could be identified.

The index to the first volume of Connecticut Colonial Records does not cover the lists of Assistants and Deputies, and the index to the second volume refers only to the page where the name of each such official first occurs. The index to the New Haven Colonial Records, though it covers the officials, is defective because of occasional omissions. The present compilation should therefore be of use both to historians and to those who wish to ascertain the services performed by their ancestors.

Considerable confusion has been caused by unfamiliarity with official titles as employed in colonial days, and by the employment of some titles in more than a single sense. To avoid this confusion, the following terms have been adopted for use herein.

Legislature is used for what was first called the General Court, and later the General Assembly.

Assistant designates a member of the Upper House of the General Court (Legislature). The term Magistrate was usual during the early years, but the title Assistant came soon into use and was employed until 1818, when the title Senator was substituted for it.

Deputy designates a member of the Lower House of the General Court (Legislature). In Connecticut the towns originally sent "Committees" to sit with the "Magistrates," but the term "Deputy" was early substituted.

Judge designates a person appointed by colonial authority to try minor cases. In Connecticut at this period they were called Commissioners, and sometimes Magistrates or Assistants. In New Haven they were usually called Deputies, but occasionally Magistrates or Constables. Since the County Courts were not established until 1666 (following the union of the two Colonies), all Judges mentioned in this work were of plantation (town) courts, except in a very few cases where they were given wider jurisdiction. Their duties were almost identical with those later discharged by Justices of the Peace.

By adopting this terminology, the ambiguity of the titles Magistrate and Deputy is avoided, and the clarity resulting from the use of standardized terms should compensate for the anachronisms involved.

Several persons who were early admitted as members of New Haven Court have been viewed erroneously as Deputies. They were merely made freemen of New Haven Court (the plantation), and were not Deputies to the Jurisdiction (Colony) Court. Hence they are omitted in the present work.

During this period there was great carelessness in recording the commissions of military officers, and the early Secretaries of Connecticut Colony were worse offenders in this respect than those of New Haven. The date of commission is stated herein when known; otherwise, the date when the title was first applied to a man in the colonial records. Since it was the General Court of the Colony which confirmed the choice of officers of commissioned rank, the use of the title in the colonial records should be considered positive proof of the legality of the commission, even though record of the appointment was not made.

In both Colonies, as soon as a regular system was adopted, Assistants served for a full year. Deputies were elected as a rule for each session, there being one in the Spring and one in the Autumn. Yet some towns in some instances elected their Deputies to serve for the entire year, and sometimes Deputies were elected to serve only at a special session. There was also a custom of electing a third man as an alternate to serve in case of the disability of either of the regular Deputies, and since special or adjourned sessions were frequent during the period covered by this compilation, three men may actually be found representing the same town within the same half-year. In listing the services of Deputies herein, *the dates of the two regular sessions are given, and those of interim sessions are omitted except for names which did not appear at the regular sessions.* These names are those of alternates or of men elected for the special session. It should also be noted that for several years Hartford, Windsor, and Wethersfield were usually represented by four instead of two deputies.

It must be remembered by those who make use of this compilation that the records of the Colony of New Haven are missing from April 1644 to May 1653 except for two Courts held in 1646. The names of Assistants and Deputies for nearly the whole of this period are therefore omitted herein, except where they have been supplied from other sources. The first volume of records relates chiefly to the plantation (town) of New Haven and not to the Colony. This has not been understood by many who have used the book, with the result that "Deputies" (Judges) of the Town Court have often been mistaken for Deputies to the General Court of the Colony.

References to volume and page of the printed records of the Colonies are made in smaller type beneath the record of each individual, to enable the reader to verify each statement. When "Shepard" is given as reference for service in the Pequot War, see the late James Shepard's "Connecticut Soldiers in the Pequot War" (Meriden, Conn., 1913); when "Mason" is given, see the Collections of the Massachusetts Historical Society, Second Series, volume VIII, pages 120 to 153.

The New Haven records stated what towns each deputy represented, but the Connecticut records of the earlier years did not do so, and often failed to state even the first names of the deputies. These deficiencies have been supplied from other sources by the editor, but the reader is asked to remember that *the names of the towns* are not given in the early Connecticut Colonial Records, and that in consequence there is some slight chance of editorial error in identifying the towns served.

Great care has been exercised to ensure accuracy, but it is too much to hope that the list is perfect. To aid identification of individuals, dates of death have been added when possible. Many of these have been taken from documentary sources, but for others we have relied upon various printed works such as town histories and family genealogies. In entering ministers, we have not attempted to distinguish between "preachers" and "teachers," but merely to indicate the dates of the connection of each minister with each parish.

The compiler expresses his appreciation of the kindness of the Connecticut Society of the Order of the Founders and Patriots of America in undertaking the publication of the List; and his gratitude to Dr. Arthur Adams of Hartford and to Roland Mather Hooker, Esq., of New Haven, for their unfailing and courteous coöperation.

LIST OF OFFICIALS
CIVIL, MILITARY, AND ECCLESIASTICAL
OF CONNECTICUT COLONY AND OF
NEW HAVEN COLONY

ALLING, ROGER (d. 1674). Corporal, New Haven Train Band, June 1652; Sergeant, Apr. 1661, confirmed July 1665 (resigned Sept. 1669). Treasurer, N. H. Col., 1661 to 1664 incl.
N. H. Town I. 131, 480. II. 250. Conn. Col. II. 23. N. H. Col. II. 403, 451, 488, 543.

ALLYN, JOHN (d. 1696). Cornet, Conn. Col. Troop, Mar. 1658; first called Lieut., Oct. 1661. Deputy (Hartford) to Conn. Leg., Oct. 1661; Assistant, Conn. Col., 1662 to 1677 incl.; Secretary, Conn. Col., 1663, 1664, 1667 to 1677 incl.; Commissioner to treat with New Haven Colony, Mar. 1663, Aug. 1663; Commissioner for United Colonies, 1674, 1675, 1677; Capt., Hartford Train Band, Oct. 1673; member of War Council, Nov. 1673, July 1675, May 1676; Indian Commissioner, May 1666; member of Militia Committee, July 1666; Commissioner to R. I., May 1668, Oct. 1668, May 1670, Oct. 1670, May 1672.
Conn. Col. I. 309, 372, 378, 384, 396, 398, 406, 407, 425. II. 13, 30, 37, 44, 57, 58, 82, 89, 103, 104, 105, 126, 134, 146, 147, 169, 173, 191, 192, 210, 219, 221, 248, 261, 274, 284, 300, 301.

ALLYN, MATTHEW (d. 1671). Deputy (Windsor) to Conn. Leg., May 1648, Oct. 1648, May 1649, Sept. 1649, May 1650, Sept. 1650, May 1651, Sept. 1651, Sept. 1654, May 1655, Oct. 1655, May 1656, Oct. 1656, Feb. 1657, Aug. 1657, Oct. 1657; Assistant, Conn. Col., 1658 to 1666 incl.; Moderator, 1666, 1667; Moderator, Conn. Col., May 1660; Patentee, Royal Charter, 1662; Commissioner to treat with New Haven Colony, Oct. 1662, Mar. 1663; Commissioner for N. Y. Boundary, Oct. 1663; Commissioner for Mass. and R. I. Boundary, Oct. 1664; Commissioner for United Colonies, May 1664; War Committee for Windsor, Oct. 1654; Committee, Stonington and Indian bounds, May 1666; Militia Committee, July 1666.
Conn. Col. I. 163, 167, 185, 195, 207, 211, 218, 224, 263, 264, 274, 278, 280, 282, 288, 300, 306, 314, 334, 347, 348, 365, 378, 384, 388, 396, 398, 410, 425, 430, 435. II. 4, 13, 30, 33, 44, 57, 60.

ALLYN, THOMAS (d. 1688). Deputy (Windsor) to Conn. Leg., May 1656.
Conn. Col. I. 281.

ALVORD, BENEDICT (d. 1683). Sergeant, granted 50 acres for service in Pequot War, May 1671. (Residence, Windsor.)
Conn. Col. II. 150.

LIST OF OFFICIALS

AMBLER, ABRAHAM (d. 1699). Deputy (Stamford), May 1674, May 1677, Oct. 1677.
Conn. Col. II. 221, 300, 318.

ANDREWS, WILLIAM (d. 1676). Sergeant, New Haven Train Band, Aug. 1642; Sergeant, Artillery Co., Mar. 1645; Lieut., Artillery Co., May 1648.
N. H. Col. I. 76, 158, 382.

ASTWOOD, JOHN (d. 1654). First called Capt., July 1646. Deputy (Milford) to N. H. Leg., Oct. 1643, Apr. 1644; Assistant, N. H. Col., Oct. 1646, May 1653, May 1654; Commissioner for United Colonies, May 1653.
N. H. Col. I. 112, 129, 263, 275. II. 1, 91.

ATWATER, JOSHUA (d. 1676). Clerk, New Haven Train Band, Aug. 1642 (resigned July 1644). Treasurer, N. H. Col., Oct. 1646, May 1653, May 1654; Judge (New Haven), June 1652, May 1653, May 1654. (Removed to Boston.)
N. H. Col. I. 75, 141, 275. II. 1, 92. N. H. Town I. 131, 180, 212.

AUGUR, NICHOLAS (d. 1676). Surgeon, N. H. Col. Troop, June 1654.
N. H. Col. II. 108.

AVERY, JAMES (d. 1700). First called Ensign, Oct. 1662; Lieut., New London Train Band, May 1665. Deputy (New London) to Conn. Leg., May 1659, Oct. 1660, Oct. 1661, May 1664, Oct. 1664, May 1665, May 1667, Oct. 1667, May 1668, May 1669, Oct. 1669, May 1675, Oct. 1675, Oct. 1676, May 1677, Oct. 1677; Judge (New London), Oct. 1663, 1664 to 1670 incl., 1674 to 1677 incl. Second Military Officer, New London County, June 1672; Capt., New London County Troop, Aug. and Nov. 1673; fifth in command, Army, King Philip's War, Nov. 1675; member of New London County Court Martial, Jan. 1677. Indian Overseer, May 1666; Committee on Indians, Oct. 1676. Granted 100 acres, May 1668; and another 100, May 1675.
Conn. Col. I. 334, 354, 372, 385, 412, 425, 426, 431. II. 13, 17, 32, 39, 58, 63, 70, 83, 84, 90, 106, 116, 131, 183, 192, 206, 218, 221, 249, 250, 257, 265, 275, 287, 300, 304, 318, 386, 484.

BACON, ANDREW (d. 1669). Deputy (Hartford) to Conn. Leg., Nov. 1637, Apr. 1642, Aug. 1642, Apr. 1643, Sept. 1643, Apr. 1644, Apr. 1646, May 1647, Sept. 1647, May 1648, Sept. 1648, May 1649, Sept. 1649, May 1650, Sept. 1650, May 1651, Sept. 1651, May 1652, Sept. 1652, May 1653, Sept. 1653, May 1654, Sept. 1654, May 1655, Oct. 1655, May 1656; War Committee for Hartford, May 1653, Oct. 1654.
Conn. Col. I. 11, 71, 73, 84, 93, 103, 138, 149, 157, 163, 166, 185, 195, 207, 211, 218, 224, 231, 235, 240, 243, 246, 256, 263, 264, 274, 278, 281.

CIVIL, MILITARY, AND ECCLESIASTICAL 3

BAKER, THOMAS (d. 1700). Assistant, Conn. Col., 1658 to 1663 incl. (Residence, Easthampton, L. I.)
Conn. Col. I. 314, 334, 347, 365, 384, 398.

BALDWIN, RICHARD (d. 1665). Ensign, N. H. Col. Troop, June 1654. Deputy (Milford) to N. H. Leg., May 1662, May 1663, Oct. 1663, Jan. 1664; Judge (Derby village), Oct. 1655.
N. H. Col. II. 108, 157, 451, 477, 488, 500, 513.

BANKS, JOHN (d. 1685). Deputy (Fairfield) to Conn. Leg., Sept. 1651, May 1661, Oct. 1663, May 1664, Oct. 1664, May 1665, Oct. 1665, May 1666, Oct. 1666, May 1673, Oct. 1673, Oct. 1674, May 1675, Oct. 1675, May 1676, Oct. 1676, May 1677, Oct. 1677; Deputy (Rye), May 1670, May 1671, May 1672, Oct. 1672, Oct. 1677; Deputy (Greenwich), Oct. 1673, May 1677, Oct. 1677; Judge (Fairfield), 1666; member of War Council, Oct. 1675, May 1676; Committee on Indians, Oct. 1676; Committee on N. Y. Boundary, Oct. 1674. Granted 100 acres, Oct. 1672.
Conn. Col. I. 224, 365, 410, 425, 431. II. 13, 24, 31, 46, 127, 147, 170, 184, 187, 192, 209, 235, 242, 249, 265, 270, 274, 284, 287, 300, 318.

BARBER, THOMAS (d. 1662). Served in Pequot War. (Residence, Windsor.)
Mason's *Narrative*.

BARNES, JOSHUA (d. after 1696). Deputy (Southampton) to Conn. Leg., May 1663.
Conn. Col. I. 399.

BARNES, THOMAS (d. 1689). Granted 50 acres, Oct. 1671 (for Pequot War service). Sergeant, Farmington Train Band, Oct. 1651.
Conn. Col. I. 227. II. 161.

BARTLETT, GEORGE (d. 1669). Sergeant, N. H. Col. Troop, June 1654; Lieut., Guilford Train Band, July 1665. Deputy (Guilford) to N. H. Leg., May 1663, Oct. 1663, May 1664. Deputy (Guilford) to Conn. Leg., May 1665.
N. H. Col. II. 108, 488, 500, 544. Conn. Col. II. 14, 22.

BASSETT, ROBERT (d. *c.* 1670). Chief Drummer, N. H. Col. Troop, June 1654. (Removed to Stamford and Hempstead.)
N. H. Col. II. 108.

BATES, JAMES (d. 1692). Deputy (Haddam), Oct. 1670, May 1671, May 1672, Oct. 1672, May 1673, May 1674. (Removed to Huntington, L. I.)
Conn. Col. II. 136, 147, 169, 184, 192, 221.

BEARD, JOHN (d. 1690). Capt., New Haven County Troop, Jan. 1676. Deputy (Milford), Oct. 1677.
Conn. Col. II. 318, 400.

BEARDSLEY, WILLIAM (d. 1661). Deputy (Stratford) to Conn. Leg., Sept. 1645, Sept. 1649, May 1650, Sept. 1651, May 1652, Oct. 1653, Feb. 1657, May 1658.
Conn. Col. I. 130, 195, 207, 224, 231, 248, 288, 315.

BECKLEY, RICHARD (d. 1690). Sergeant, New Haven Artillery Co., May 1648. (Removed to Wethersfield.) Granted 300 acres, Oct. 1668.
N. H. Col. I. 382. Conn. Col. II. 100.

BEEBE, JOHN (d. 1714). Ensign, New London County Troop, May 1676.
Conn. Col. II. 279.

BELL, ABRAHAM (d. 1662-3). Corporal, New Haven Train Band, July 1644 (resigned Mar. 1645). (Removed to Charlestown, Mass.)
N. H. Col. I. 141, 160.

BELL, FRANCIS (d. 1690). Lieut., Stamford Train Band, May 1655; also, Oct. 1666. Deputy (Stamford) to N. H. Leg., May 1653, May 1654, May 1655, May 1656, May 1657, May 1658, May 1659, May 1661, May 1662, May 1663, Jan. 1664, May 1664; Judge (Stamford), May 1652, May 1654, May 1655, May 1656, May 1658, May 1659, May 1660, May 1661, May 1662, May 1663.
N. H. Col. II. 2, 92, 96, 141, 145, 148, 169, 172, 214, 232, 235, 297, 304, 369, 403, 405, 451, 453, 488, 489, 513, 544. Conn. Col. II. 55.

BELL, JONATHAN (d. 1699). Deputy (Stamford), Oct. 1670, May 1674, Oct. 1675, May 1676, Oct. 1676, May 1677. Called Lieut., May 1674.
Conn. Col. II. 136, 221, 265, 274, 286, 300.

BENEDICT, THOMAS (d. 1690). Judge (Jamaica), May 1664; Deputy (Norwalk), May 1670, May 1675.
Conn. Col. I. 428. II. 127, 249.

BETTS, JOHN (d. 1690). Sergeant, Wethersfield Train Band, May 1657. (Removed to Huntington, L. I.)
Conn. Col. I. 299.

BETTS, RICHARD (d. 1713). Judge (Newtown), May 1664.
Conn. Col. I. 428.

BIDWELL, JOHN, JR. (d. 1692). Grant of 200 acres to him and Bull for sawmill, May 1669.
Conn. Col. II. 111.

BIRCHARD [BIRCHWOOD], JOHN (d. 1702). Judge (Norwich), Oct. 1676, May 1677.
Conn. Col. II. 292, 304.

BIRCHARD [BURCHARD], THOMAS (d. after 1683). Deputy

CIVIL, MILITARY, AND ECCLESIASTICAL 5

(Saybrook) to Conn. Leg., May 1650, May 1651. (Removed to Edgartown, Mass.)
Conn. Col. I. 207, 218.

BISHOP, JAMES (d. 1691). Corporal, New Haven Train Band, Aug. 1657; Sergeant, confirmed July 1665 (resigned Aug. 1665). Deputy (New Haven) to N. H. Leg., Aug. 1661, May 1662, Nov. 1662, May 1663, Oct. 1663, Jan. 1664; Secretary, N. H. Col., 1661 to 1664 incl.; Deputy (New Haven) to Conn. Leg., Apr. 1665, May 1665, Oct. 1665, May 1666, Oct. 1666, May 1667, Oct. 1667; Judge (New Haven), 1661 to 1667 incl.; Assistant, 1668 to 1677 incl.; Clerk of New Haven County Court, May 1666; Committee on Indians, May 1668; member of War Council, Nov. 1673, July 1675, May 1676. Granted 300 acres, Oct. 1669.
N. H. Col. II. 403, 418, 451, 488, 500, 513, 543. N. H. Town I. 321, 484, 485, 521, 523. II. 15, 40, 45, 89, 140, 142, 145, 155. Conn. Col. I. 439. II. 13, 18, 23, 31, 32, 38, 46, 58, 63, 69, 82, 104, 123, 126, 146, 169, 191, 219, 221, 248, 261, 274, 284, 300.

BISHOP, JOHN (REV.) (d. 1695). Minister at Stamford, 1644–1695. Granted 200 acres, Oct. 1674.
Conn. Col. II. 241.

BISSELL, JOHN, SR. (d. 1677). Deputy (Windsor) to Conn. Leg., May 1648, Sept. 1648, May 1650, Sept. 1650, Sept. 1651, May 1652, Sept. 1652, May 1653, Sept. 1653, May 1654, Sept. 1654, May 1655, Oct. 1655, May 1658, Oct. 1658, May 1664. Granted 100 acres, May 1674.
Conn. Col. I. 163, 166, 207, 211, 224, 231, 235, 240, 246, 256, 264, 274, 278, 315, 323, 425. II. 230.

BISSELL, JOHN, JR. (d. 1688).* Quartermaster, Hartford County Troop, May 1677.
Conn. Col. II. 311. III. 91, 450.
*Stiles' History of Ancient Windsor, II, 77 is in error; it was John Bissell, 3d, who d. 1693.

BISSELL, SAMUEL (d. 1700). Deputy (Windsor) to Conn. Leg., Mar. 1656.
Conn. Col. I. 279.

BLACKLEACH, JOHN, JR. (d. 1703). Granted 200 acres, Oct. 1674. (Residence, Wethersfield.)
Conn. Col. II. 240.

BLACKMAN, ADAM (REV.) (d. 1665). Minister at Stratford, 1640–1665.

BLATCHFORD, PETER (d. 1671). Deputy (Haddam), May 1669, May 1670. Heirs granted 50 acres, Oct. 1671 (for Pequot War service).
Conn. Col. II. 105, 127, 161.

BLATCHLEY, THOMAS (d. 1674). Deputy (Branford), May 1667, Oct. 1668, Oct. 1669, May 1670, Oct. 1670, May 1671, Oct. 1671, May

1672, Oct. 1672. Granted 60 acres, May 1670 (for Pequot War service).
Conn. Col. II. 58, 94, 116, 127, 133, 136, 147, 160, 169, 184.

BLINMAN, RICHARD (REV.) (d. 1679–83). Minister at Marshfield, Mass., 1642; at Gloucester, Mass., 1642–1650; at New London, 1650–1658. (Returned to England, 1659.)

BLUMFIELD, WILLIAM. Served in Pequot War. (Removed to Newtown, L. I.) Lot in Soldiers' Field, Hartford.

BOARDMAN, SAMUEL (d. 1673). Deputy (Wethersfield) to Conn. Leg., Oct. 1657, May 1658, Oct. 1658, May 1659, Oct. 1659, May 1660, Oct. 1660, May 1661, Oct. 1661, May 1662, Oct. 1662, May 1663, Oct. 1663, May 1664, Oct. 1664, May 1665, May 1667, Oct. 1671.
Conn. Col. I. 306, 315, 323, 334, 340, 347, 354, 365, 372, 378, 384, 399, 409, 425, 431. II. 13, 58, 159.

BOND, ROBERT (d. 1677). Assistant, Conn. Col., May 1659, May 1660, May 1661; Judge (Easthampton), May 1663, May 1664. (Removed to Elizabethtown, N. J.)
Conn. Col. I. 334, 347, 365, 400, 428.

BOOSY, JAMES (d. 1649). Clerk, Wethersfield Train Band, Apr. 1645; first called Lieut., Sept. 1647. Deputy (Wethersfield) to Conn. Leg., Apr. 1639, Aug. 1639, Jan. 1640, Apr. 1640, Feb. 1641, Apr. 1641, Apr. 1642, Sept. 1643, Apr. 1644, Sept. 1644, Apr. 1645, Sept. 1645, Apr. 1646, Oct. 1646, May 1647, Sept. 1647, May 1648, Sept. 1648, May 1649.
Conn. Col. I. 27, 29, 34, 41, 46, 58, 64, 71, 93, 103, 111, 124, 125, 130, 138, 145, 149, 157, 163, 166, 185.

BOTSFORD, HENRY (d. 1686). Corporal, N. H. Col. Troop, June 1654. (Residence, Milford.)
N. H. Col. II. 109.

BOUTON, JOHN (d. 1707). Deputy (Norwalk), Oct. 1669, Oct. 1671, Oct. 1673, May 1674, May 1675, Oct. 1676, May 1677, Oct. 1677.
Conn. Col. II. 116, 159, 209, 221, 249, 286, 300, 318.

BOWERS, JOHN (REV.) (d. 1687). Teacher at New Haven, 1656–1660; preacher at Guilford, 1660–1664; at Branford, 1667–1672; minister at Derby, 1673–1687.

BOYKIN, JARVIS (d. *c.* 1660). Corporal, New Haven Train Band, May 1652; Corporal, N. H. Col. Troop, June 1654; Sergeant, Train Band, Aug. 1657.
N. H. Town I. 127, 321. N. H. Col. II. 109.

BRADLEY, WILLIAM (d. 1691). Deputy (New Haven), Oct. 1675, May 1676.
Conn. Col. II. 265, 274.

CIVIL, MILITARY, AND ECCLESIASTICAL

BRADSTREET, SIMON (d. 1683). Harvard College, 1660. Minister at New London, 1666–1683. Granted 200 acres, Oct. 1673.
Conn. Col. II. 214.

BREWSTER, BENJAMIN (d. 1710). Deputy (Norwich), May 1668; Lieut., New London County Troop, Oct. 1673. Granted 200 acres, May 1668.
Conn. Col. II. 83, 90, 213.

BREWSTER, JONATHAN (d. 1659). Deputy (New London) to Conn. Leg., Sept. 1650, May 1655, May 1656, May 1657, Oct. 1657, May 1658, Oct. 1658; Judge (New London), May 1657.
Conn. Col. I. 211, 274, 281, 297, 298, 306, 315, 323.

BRINSMADE, JOHN (d. 1673). Deputy (Stratford), Oct. 1671, May 1672, Oct. 1672.
Conn. Col. II. 159, 170, 184.

BROCKETT, JOHN (d. 1690). Surgeon, N. H. Col. Troop, June 1654. (Residence, New Haven.) Deputy (Wallingford), Oct. 1671, May 1672, Oct. 1673, Oct. 1674, May 1675; Judge (Wallingford), 1672; Surgeon, King Philip's War, Jan. and May 1676.
N. H. Col. II. 108. Conn. Col. II. 160, 169, 170, 209, 236, 249, 286, 399.

BRONSON, JOHN (d. 1680). Served in Pequot War. Deputy (Farmington) to Conn. Leg., May 1651, Oct. 1655, May 1656, Oct. 1656.
Conn. Col. I. 218, 278, 281, 283.

BROWN, FRANCIS (d. 1686). Deputy (Stamford) to Conn. Leg., May 1665, May 1667, Oct. 1668, May 1669.
Conn. Col. II. 14, 59, 95, 106.

BRUEN, OBADIAH (d. after 1680). Patentee, Royal Charter, 1662; Dep. Judge (New London), Apr. 1660, May 1660; Judge (New London), 1662 to 1666 incl.; Deputy (New London) to Conn. Leg., Oct. 1665, Oct. 1666; Clerk, New London County Court, May 1666.
Conn. Col. I. 347, 352, 382, 402, 412, 426. II. 4, 17, 24, 32, 38, 47.

BRUNDAGE, JOHN (d. 1697). Deputy (Rye), May 1677.
Conn. Col. II. 300.

BRYAN, ALEXANDER (d. 1679). First called Ensign (Milford Train Band), Feb. 1650; confirmed Ensign, July 1665. Judge (Milford), 1666, 1667; Assistant, 1668 to 1677 incl.; member of War Council, Nov. 1673, July 1675, May 1676.
N. H. Town I. 2. Conn. Col. II. 21, 31, 63, 82, 104, 126, 146, 169, 191, 219, 221, 248, 261, 274, 284, 300. See also N. H. Col. II. 28, 486, etc.

BUCKINGHAM, DANIEL (d. 1712). Confirmed Sergeant, Milford Train Band, July 1665.
Conn. Col. II. 21.

BUCKINGHAM, SAMUEL (d. 1700). Deputy for Milford, Oct. 1675.
Conn. Col. II. 265.

BUCKINGHAM, THOMAS (d. 1657). Deputy (Milford) to N. H. Leg., May 1656.
N. H. Col. II. 169.

BUCKINGHAM, THOMAS (REV.) (d. 1709). Minister at Wethersfield, 1664; at Saybrook, 1670–1709.

BUCKLAND, THOMAS (d. 1662). Grant to his heirs of 50 acres, Oct. 1671 (for Pequot War service). (Residence, Windsor.)
Conn. Col. II. 161.

BUDD, JOHN (d. c. 1684). Lieut., Southold Train Band, prior to May 1654. Deputy (Southold) to N. H. Leg., May 1657; Judge (Southold), May 1657. Deputy (Hastings) to Conn. Leg., Oct. 1664; Judge (Hastings), Oct. 1663, (Hastings and Rye), Oct. 1664, (Rye), May 1666, May 1667, Oct. 1668.
N. H. Col. II. 97, 214, 215. Conn. Col. I. 413, 431, 436. II. 31, 59, 94.

BULKELEY, GERSHOM (REV.) (d. 1713). Harvard College, 1655. Minister at New London, 1661–1665; at Wethersfield, 1667–1676. Chirurgeon to Army and added to War Council, Oct. 1675; with army, Dec. 1675, Feb. and May 1676.
Conn. Col. II. 271, 279, 388, 409, 483.

BULL, JIREH (d. 1684). Judge (Kingston, R. I.), May 1673.
Conn. Col. II. 198.

BULL, JOSEPH (d. 1712). Grant of 200 acres to him and Bidwell for sawmill, May 1669. (Residence, Hartford.)
Conn. Col. II. 111.

BULL, THOMAS (d. 1684). First called Lieut., Oct. 1651; Lieut., Conn. Col. Troop, May 1653. Capt., Hartford County Troop, Nov. 1673; Capt., King Philip's War, July and Sept. 1675. Granted 200 acres, May 1673 (for service in Pequot War). (Residence, Hartford.)
Conn. Col. I. 228, 230, 242. II. 199, 218, 333, 369.

BUNCE, THOMAS (d. 1683). Granted 60 acres for service in Pequot War, May 1671, and 50 acres more, Oct. 1672. (Residence, Hartford.)
Conn. Col. II. 154, 187.

BURCHARD, see BIRCHARD.

BURR, BENJAMIN (d. 1681). Served in Pequot War. (Residence, Hartford.)
Shepard.

BURR, JEHU (d. c. 1650). Collector (Springfield), Feb. 1638. Deputy (Springfield) to Conn. Leg., Apr. 1638; Deputy (Fairfield) to Conn. Leg., Sept. 1641, Sept. 1645, Apr. 1646.
Conn. Col. I. 12, 17, 67, 130, 138.

CIVIL, MILITARY, AND ECCLESIASTICAL 9

BURR, JEHU (d. 1692). Deputy (Fairfield) to Conn. Leg., Oct. 1659, Oct. 1660, May 1661, May 1663, Oct. 1663, May 1668, Oct. 1668, May 1669, May 1670, Oct. 1670, May 1672, May 1673, Oct. 1673, May 1674, May 1675, Oct. 1675, May 1676; Judge (Fairfield), 1664, 1668 to 1677 incl.; Lieut., Fairfield County Troop, Aug. 1673; member of War Council, Oct. 1675, May 1676. Granted 200 acres, May 1673.
Conn. Col. I. 340, 354, 365, 399, 410, 426. II. 83, 84, 94, 105, 106, 127, 131, 136, 152, 170, 192, 193, 200, 206, 209, 221, 249, 250, 265, 270, 274, 276, 284, 304.

BURR, JOHN (d. 1694). Deputy (Fairfield), May 1666, Oct. 1667, May 1670, Oct. 1670, May 1671, Oct. 1671, May 1674.
Conn. Col. II. 31, 70, 127, 136, 147, 159, 221.

BURRITT, STEPHEN (d. 1698). Ensign, Stratford Train Band, June 1672; Ensign, Fairfield County Dragoons, Sept. 1675; Commissary of Army, Nov. 1675; Lieut., Fairfield County Troop, Jan. 1675.
Conn. Col. II. 181, 367, 384, 400.

BURWELL, SAMUEL (d. 1715). Ensign, New Haven County Troop, May 1676. (Residence, Milford.)
Conn. Col. II. 279.

BUSHNELL, WILLIAM (d. 1683). Sergeant, Saybrook Train Band, Oct. 1661. Deputy (Saybrook), May 1670.
Conn. Col. I. 375. II. 127.

BUTLER, RICHARD (d. 1684). Deputy (Hartford) to Conn. Leg., Oct. 1656, May 1657, Oct. 1657, May 1658, Oct. 1658, May 1659, Oct. 1659, May 1660.
Conn. Col. I. 282, 297, 306, 315, 323, 334, 340, 347.

BUTLER, SAMUEL. Deputy (Farmington?), May 1668.
Conn. Col. II. 82. [Samuel of Wethersfield d. 1692.]

CALKINS, HUGH (d. 1690). Deputy (New London) to Conn. Leg., May 1652, May 1653, Oct. 1653, May 1654, Sept. 1654, May 1656, Oct. 1656, Oct. 1657, May 1658, May 1659, May 1660; Deputy (Norwich) to Conn. Leg., Mar. 1663, May 1663, May 1664, May 1665, May 1666, Oct. 1666, May 1669, Oct. 1669, Oct. 1671; War Committee for New London, May 1653, Oct. 1654.
Conn. Col. I. 231, 240, 243, 248, 256, 264, 281, 283, 306, 315, 334, 347, 392, 399, 425. II. 14, 31, 47, 106, 116, 169.

CAMP, NICHOLAS (d. 1706). Deputy (Milford), Oct. 1670, May 1671, Oct. 1671, May 1672, Oct. 1672.
Conn. Col. II. 136, 147, 160, 169, 184.

CANFIELD, MATTHEW (d. 1673). Deputy (Norwalk) to Conn. Leg., May 1654, May 1655, May 1656, May 1657, May 1658, May 1659, May 1660, May 1661, May 1662, Oct. 1662, Oct. 1663, May 1664, Oct. 1664, May 1665, Oct. 1665, May 1666, Oct. 1666; Patentee,

LIST OF OFFICIALS

Royal Charter, 1662; Judge (Norwalk), 1654 to 1657 incl., 1661, 1667. (Removed to Newark, N. J.)
  Conn. Col. I. 256, 257, 274, 281, 297, 300, 315, 334, 347, 365, 379, 384, 410, 425, 432. II. 4, 14, 24, 31, 47, 63.

CANFIELD, THOMAS (d. 1689). Sergeant, Milford Train Band, May 1669; Deputy (Milford), Oct. 1673, Oct. 1674, Oct. 1676.
  Conn. Col. II. 107, 209, 236, 286.

CASE, JOHN (d. 1704). Constable (Simsbury), Oct. 1669; Deputy (Simsbury), May 1670, Oct. 1674, May 1675.
  Conn. Col. II. 118, 126, 236, 249.

CAULKINS, see CALKINS.

CHADWICK [CHADDUCK], JAMES. Commissary, King Philip's War, Jan. 1677. (He was of Malden, Mass.)
  Conn. Col. II. 484.

CHAPLIN, CLEMENT. Deputy (Wethersfield) to Conn. Leg., May 1637, Mar. 1643, Apr. 1643, Sept. 1643; Treasurer, Conn. Col., Feb. 1638.
  Conn. Col. I. 9, 12, 82, 84, 93.

CHAPMAN, ROBERT (d. 1687). Served in the Pequot War. Deputy (Saybrook) to Conn. Leg., Sept. 1652, May 1653, Sept. 1653, Sept. 1654, Feb. 1657, Aug. 1657, Oct. 1657, May 1658, Oct. 1658, May 1659, Oct. 1659, May 1660, Oct. 1660, Oct. 1661, May 1662, Oct. 1662, May 1663, Oct. 1663, Oct. 1664, May 1665, May 1667, Oct. 1667, May 1668, Oct. 1668, May 1669, Oct. 1669, May 1670, Oct. 1670, May 1671, Oct. 1671, May 1674, May 1675, Oct. 1675, Oct. 1676, May 1677, Oct. 1677; Judge (Saybrook), 1660 to 1677 incl.; War Committee for Saybrook, May 1653, Oct. 1654; Committee on Indians, May 1668; Capt., Saybrook Train Band, Oct. 1675.
  Conn. Col. I. 235, 240, 243, 246, 264, 288, 300, 306, 315, 323, 334, 340, 347, 351, 354, 365, 372, 379, 384, 399, 410, 426, 431. II. 14, 17, 32, 63, 70, 83, 84, 88, 94, 105, 106, 116, 127, 131, 136, 147, 152, 159, 170, 192, 221, 249, 250, 265, 269, 275, 286, 300, 304, 318. Lyon Gardiner's *Relation of the Pequot Wars.*

CHAPMAN, THOMAS.* Deputy (Saybrook) to Conn. Leg., May 1652.
  Conn. Col. I. 231.
  *Error for Robert?

CHAPPELL, GEORGE (d. 1709). Granted 50 acres, Oct. 1670. (Served in the Pequot War; residence, New London.)
  Conn. Col. II. 144.

CHAUNCEY, ISRAEL (REV.) (d. 1703). Minister at Stratford, 1665–1703. Chaplain, King Philip's War, and member of Council of War, Oct. 1675.
  Conn. Col. II. 267, 271.

CHAUNCEY, NATHANIEL (REV.) (d. 1685). Harvard College, 1661. Minister at Windsor, 1667–1679; at Hatfield, Mass., 1680–1685.

CHEEVER, EZEKIEL (d. 1708). Deputy (New Haven) to N. H. Leg., Apr. 1646, Oct. 1646. (Removed to Boston.)
N. H. Col. I. 227, 274.

CHENEY, WILLIAM (d. 1705). Deputy (Middletown) to Conn. Leg., May 1660, Oct. 1660, May 1662, Oct. 1663, Oct. 1664, Oct. 1667, May 1670, May 1672, Oct. 1672, Oct. 1673, Oct. 1675, May 1676, May 1677; called Sergeant, Oct. 1675; Ensign Middletown Train Band, May 1677.
Conn. Col. I. 347, 354, 379, 410, 431. II. 70, 126, 184, 209, 265, 274, 300, 304.

CHESEBROUGH, ELISHA (d: 1727). Deputy (Stonington), Oct. 1669.
Conn. Col. II. 116.

CHESEBROUGH, SAMUEL (d. 1673). Deputy (Stonington), May 1665, May 1666, Oct. 1666, May 1670, May 1671, May 1672, May 1673.
Conn. Col. II. 14, 31, 47, 127, 147, 170, 192.

CHESEBROUGH, WILLIAM (d. 1667). Deputy (New London) to Conn. Leg., May 1653, Sept. 1653, Sept. 1654, May 1655, Feb. 1657; Deputy (Stonington), Oct. 1664; Judge (Stonington town), Oct. 1664; Indian Overseer, May 1666.
Conn. Col. I. 240, 246, 264, 274, 288, 432, 435. II. 39.

CHESTER, "MR." (not identified). War Committee for Windsor, May 1653.
Conn. Col. I. 243.

CHESTER, JOHN (d. 1698). Lieut., Wethersfield Train Band, May 1672; called Capt., Oct. 1676; Capt., Wethersfield Train Band, May 1677; Deputy (Wethersfield), May 1676, Oct. 1676, May 1677, Oct. 1677; Judge (Wethersfield), 1676, 1677. Granted 200 acres, May 1673.
Conn. Col. II. 172, 200, 274, 275, 286, 300, 304, 305, 318.

CHITTENDEN, WILLIAM (d. 1661). Sergeant, New Haven Artillery Co., May 1648; first called Lieut., Oct. 1653. Deputy (Guilford) to N. H. Leg., May 1653, May 1654, May 1655, May 1656, May 1657, May 1658, May 1659.
N. H. Col. I. 382. II. 2, 36, 92, 141, 169, 214, 232, 297.

CLARK, DANIEL (d. 1710). Deputy (Windsor) to Conn. Leg., Oct. 1653, Oct. 1656, Feb. 1657, Aug. 1657, Oct. 1657, May 1658, May 1659, Oct. 1659, May 1661; Assistant, Conn. Col., 1662, 1663, 1664, 1666, 1667; Secretary, Conn. Col., May 1658, May 1659, May 1660, May 1661, May 1662, Oct. 1662, May 1663 (removed), May 1665, May 1666; Patentee, Royal Charter, 1662; Commissioner to treat with N. H.

Col., Aug. 1663; Commissioner on N. Y. Boundary, Oct. 1663. Lieut., Conn. Col. Troop, Mar. 1658; Capt. of same, May 1664. Committee, Stonington and Indian bounds, May 1666; Militia Committee, July 1666; member of Council of War, May 1676; Clerk, Hartford County Court, May 1666.

Conn. Col. I. 248, 282, 288, 300, 306, 309, 315, 334, 340, 347, 365, 378, 384, 398, 407, 410, 425, 429. II. 4, 13, 30, 33, 38, 44, 58, 284.

CLARK, GEORGE (DEACON) (d. 1690). Deputy (Milford) to N. H. Leg., May 1664. Deputy (Milford) to Conn. Leg., Apr. 1665, May 1666, May 1668, Oct. 1668, May 1669, Oct. 1669, May 1672, May 1673, May 1674, Oct. 1674, May 1675, Oct. 1675, May 1676, Oct. 1677 (then called Deacon Jn° by error).

N. H. Col. II. 544. Conn. Col. I. 439. II. 31, 83, 94, 105, 115, 169, 192, 221, 236, 249, 265, 274, 286.

CLARK, HENRY (d. *c.* 1675). Deputy (Windsor) to Conn. Leg., Sept. 1641, Apr. 1642, Aug. 1642, Mar. 1643, Sept. 1644, Oct. 1646, May 1647, Sept. 1647, Sept. 1648, May 1649, Sept. 1649; Assistant, Conn. Col., May 1650, May 1651, May 1652, May 1653, May 1654, May 1655, May 1656 (erroneously called John), May 1657, May 1658, May 1659, May 1660, May 1661; Patentee, Royal Charter, 1662; War Committee for Windsor, May 1653. (Removed to Hadley, Mass.)

Conn. Col. I. 67, 71, 73, 82, 111, 145, 149, 157, 166, 185, 195, 207, 218, 231, 240, 243, 256, 274, 280, 297, 314, 334, 347, 364. II. 4.

CLARK, JOHN (d. 1649). Served in the Pequot War. Sergeant, New Haven Train Band, Aug. 1642 (resigned July 1644); Clerk of same, Feb. 1648.

N. H. Col. I. 76, 141, 370.

CLARK, JOHN (d. 1674). Served in the Pequot War; War Committee for Saybrook, May 1653, Oct. 1654; Deputy (Saybrook) to Conn. Leg., May 1649, May 1651, Sept. 1651, May 1652, May 1653, Sept. 1653, July 1654, Sept. 1654, May 1655, May 1656, Oct. 1656, Feb. 1657, Aug. 1657, Oct. 1657, May 1658, Oct. 1658, May 1659, Oct. 1659, May 1661, Oct. 1661, May 1662, Oct. 1662, May 1663; Deputy (Milford) to Conn. Leg., Apr. 1665, May 1665, Oct. 1666, May 1667, Oct. 1667, Oct. 1668; Patentee, Royal Charter, 1662; Judge (Saybrook), May 1664; Judge (Milford), 1665 to 1673 incl.

Conn. Col. I. 185, 218, 224, 231, 240, 243, 246, 261, 264, 274, 281, 282, 288, 300, 306, 315, 323, 334, 340, 365, 372, 379, 384, 399, 426, 439. II. 4, 13, 17, 23, 32, 46, 58, 63, 69, 94, 106, 131, 152, 170, 193.

CLARK, NICHOLAS (d. 1680). Granted 50 acres, Oct. 1671 (for service in Pequot War). (Residence, Hartford).

Conn. Col. II. 161.

CIVIL, MILITARY, AND ECCLESIASTICAL 13

COE, JOHN (d. c. 1693). Judge (Newtown), May 1664; called Capt. same date.
Conn. Col. I. 428.

COE, ROBERT (d. 1672). Dep. Judge (Stamford), Apr. 1643; Deputy (Stamford) to N. H. Leg., Apr. 1644; Judge (Jamaica), May 1664.
N. H. Col. I. 85, 129. Conn. Col. I. 428.

COLE, JOHN (d. 1685). Deputy (Farmington) to Conn. Leg., Oct. 1653, May 1654.
Conn. Col. I. 248, 256.

COLE, JOHN (d. 1707). Judge (Wickford), Oct. 1670, May 1671.
Conn. Col. II. 138, 157.

COLEMAN, THOMAS (d. 1674). Deputy (Wethersfield) to Conn. Leg., Oct. 1650, May 1651, May 1652, Sept. 1652, May 1653, Sept. 1653, May 1654, Sept. 1654, Oct. 1655, May 1656; War Committee for Wethersfield, Oct. 1654. (Removed to Hadley.)
Conn. Col. I. 212, 218, 231, 235, 240, 246, 256, 264, 278, 281.

COLLINS, NATHANIEL (REV.) (d. 1684). Harvard College, 1660. Minister at Middletown, 1668–1684.

COLLINS, SAMUEL (d. 1696). Deputy (Middletown), Oct. 1674.
Conn. Col. II. 184.

COMSTOCK, WILLIAM. Served in Pequot War. (Removed to New London.)
Shepard.

COOKE, AARON (d. 1690). Lieut. (Commanding), Conn. Col. Troop, May 1653; called Capt., Mar. 1658.
Conn. Col. I. 242, 309.

COOKE, THOMAS (d. 1692). Deputy (Guilford) to Conn. Leg., Apr. 1665, May 1666.
Conn. Col. I. 439. II. 31.

COOPER, JOHN (d. 1689). Corporal, N. H. Col. Troop, June 1654. Deputy (New Haven) to N. H. Leg., May 1661, Aug. 1661, May 1662, Nov. 1662. Deputy (New Haven) to Conn. Leg., Apr. 1665, Oct. 1665, Oct. 1666, May 1671, Oct. 1671, Oct. 1674. Judge (New Haven), May 1661.
N. H. Col. II. 109, 403, 418, 451. Conn. Col. I. 439. II. 23, 46, 147, 160, 235. N. H. Town I. 484, 485, 521. II. 15, 137, 140, 155.

CORNWALL, WILLIAM (d. 1678). Served in the Pequot War. Deputy (Middletown) to Conn. Leg., May 1654, Oct. 1664; called Sergeant on the latter date.
Conn. Col. I. 256, 431.

COSMORE, see GOSMER.

COTTON, JOHN (REV.) (d. 1699). Harvard College, 1657. Preacher at Wethersfield, 1660–1663, and at Guilford for a time; removed.

CRABBE, RICHARD (d. 1680). Deputy (Wethersfield) to Conn. Leg., Apr. 1639, Jan. 1640, Apr. 1640, Feb. 1641, Apr. 1641. (Removed to Stamford and Oyster Bay.)
Conn. Col. I. 27, 41, 46, 58, 64.

CRANE, HENRY (d. 1711). Deputy (Killingworth), May 1675, May 1676, May 1677; called Lieut., May 1676; Lieut., Killingworth Train Band, Oct. 1676.
Conn. Col. II. 249, 274, 292, 300.

CRANE, JASPER (d. 1681). Deputy (New Haven) to N. H. Col. Leg., May 1648, May 1649, Sept. 1649, May 1650; Deputy (Branford) to N. H. Col. Leg., May 1653, May 1654, May 1655, May 1656, May 1657; Judge (New Haven), Oct. 1645, Oct. 1646, Oct. 1647, May 1648, May 1649, May 1650; Judge (Branford), May 1654, May 1655, May 1656, May 1657; Assistant, N. H. Col., May 1658, May 1659, May 1660, May 1661, May 1662, May 1663, May 1664; Assistant (provisional appointment, Conn. Col.), Oct. 1664; Assistant, Conn. Col., 1665, 1666, 1667. (Removed to Newark, N. J.)
N. H. Col. I. 173, 274, 354, 381, 456, 481. II. 2, 92, 96, 141, 148, 169, 172, 214, 215, 231, 297, 359, 402, 451, 488, 543. Conn. Col. I. 437. II. 13, 30, 58. N. H. Town I. 21.

CULLICK, JOHN (d. 1663). Served in the Pequot War. Deputy (Hartford) to Conn. Leg., Sept. 1644, Oct. 1646, May 1647; Assistant, Conn. Col., May 1648, May 1649, May 1650, May 1651, May 1652, May 1653, May 1654, May 1655, May 1656, May 1657; Secretary, Conn. Col., May 1648, May 1649, May 1650, May 1652, May 1654, May 1655, May 1656, May 1657; Commissioner for United Colonies, May 1652, May 1653, June 1654, May 1655. First called Capt., May 1653.
Conn. Col. I. 111, 145, 149, 163, 185, 207, 218, 231, 233, 240, 241, 256, 274, 280, 297.

CULVER, EDWARD (d. 1685). Scout, King Philip's War, Feb. 1676. (Residence, New London.)
Conn. Col. II. 408.

CURTIS, WILLIAM (d. 1702). Deputy (Stratford), Oct. 1667, May 1668, Oct. 1668, May 1669, Oct. 1669, May 1670, Oct. 1670, May 1671 (called Lieut. Joseph by error), May 1672, Oct. 1672, May 1673, Oct. 1673, May 1674, Oct. 1674, May 1675, Oct. 1675, Oct. 1676, May 1677, Oct. 1677; Judge (Stratford), 1671, 1672, 1673, 1674, 1675, (Stratford and Woodbury), 1676, 1677; called Lieut., Oct. 1667; Capt., Stratford Train Band, June 1672; Second Military Officer, Fairfield County, June 1672; Capt., Fairfield County Troop, Nov. 1673, Oct.

1675; Militia Committee, June 1672; War Committee, Aug. 1673.
Conn. Col. II. 70, 83, 94, 105, 116, 127, 136, 147, 152, 170, 181, 183, 184, 192, 193, 204, 209, 218, 221, 236, 249, 250, 265, 268, 276, 286, 300, 304, 318.

DAVENPORT, JOHN (REV.) (d. 1670). Minister at New Haven, 1639-1668; at Boston, 1668-1670.

DAVENPORT, JOHN, JR. (d. 1676). Judge (New Haven), Nov. 1660, May 1661 (declined), June 1662, May 1663, May 1664, 1666, 1667.
N. H. Town I. 463, 484, 523. II. 45, 89. Conn. Col. II. 32, 63.

DAVIS, PHILIP (d. 1689). Served in Pequot War. (Residence, Hartford.)
Mason's *Narrative*.

DEMING, JOHN (d. *c*. 1694). Deputy (Wethersfield) to Conn. Leg., Dec. 1645, Oct. 1646, Sept. 1649, May 1650, May 1651, Sept. 1651, May 1652, Sept. 1652, Oct. 1653, May 1655, Oct. 1656, Feb. 1657, May 1657, May 1658, Oct. 1658, May 1659, Oct. 1659, May 1660, Oct. 1660, May 1661, Oct. 1661, Oct. 1667, May 1668, Oct. 1668, May 1669, Oct. 1672. Patentee, Royal Charter, 1662.
Conn. Col. I. 133, 145, 195, 207, 218, 224, 231, 235, 248, 274, 282, 288, 297, 315, 323, 334, 340, 347, 354, 365, 372. II. 4, 69, 82, 94, 105, 183.

DENISON, GEORGE (d. 1694). Deputy (New London) to Conn. Leg., Sept. 1653, May 1654, Feb. 1657; Deputy (Stonington), Oct. 1671, Oct. 1674, May 1675. First called Capt., May 1653; War Committee for New London, May 1653, Oct. 1654; Capt. in King Philip's War, Feb. and Apr. 1676; Capt., New London County Troop, and second in command of Army, May 1676; Capt., Aug. 1676; Provost Marshal, May 1677.
Conn. Col. I. 243, 246, 256, 264, 288. II. 159, 236, 249, 279, 306, 407, 429, 468.

DENISON, JOHN (d. 1698). Ensign, New London County Troop, Aug. 1673.
Conn. Col. II. 206.

DENTON, RICHARD (d. 1663). Minister at Stamford, 1641-1644; at Hempstead, L. I., 1644-1663.

DICKERMAN, ABRAHAM (d. 1711). Corporal, New Haven Train Band, July 1665.
N. H. Town II. 144.

DICKINSON, JOHN (d. 1676). Sergeant, Wethersfield Train Band, May 1657. (Removed to Hadley.)
Conn. Col. I. 299.

DICKINSON, NATHANIEL (d. 1676). Deputy (Wethersfield) to Conn. Leg., Apr. 1646, Oct. 1646, May 1647, Sept. 1647, May 1648, Dec. 1648, May 1649, Sept. 1649, May 1650, Sept. 1650, May 1651, Sept. 1651, May 1652, Sept. 1652, May 1653, Sept. 1653, Sept. 1654,

May 1655, Oct. 1655, May 1656; War Committee for Wethersfield, May 1653, Oct. 1654. (Removed to Hadley.)
> Conn. Col. I. 138, 145, 149, 157, 163, 170, 185, 195, 207, 211, 218, 224, 231, 235, 240, 243, 246, 264, 274, 278, 281.

DISBOROUGH, NICHOLAS (d. 1683). Granted 50 acres, May 1671 (for service in Pequot War). (Residence, Hartford.)
> Conn. Col. II. 149.

DISBOROUGH, SAMUEL (d. 1690). Deputy (Guilford) to N. H. Leg., Oct. 1643; Assistant, N. H. Col., Oct. 1646. (Returned to England.)
> N. H. Col. I. 112, 275.

DISBROW, PETER (d. 1688). Deputy (Rye) to Conn. Leg., May 1665, May 1670, May 1671, May 1673, May 1676.
> Conn. Col. II. 14, 127, 147, 192, 274.

DOOLITTLE, ABRAHAM (d. 1690). Corporal, New Haven Train Band, Aug. 1657; Sergeant of same, July 1665. Marshal, N. H. Col., May 1662, May 1663, May 1664. Deputy (New Haven), Oct. 1668; Deputy (Wallingford), May 1671, Oct. 1672.
> N. H. Town I. 321. II. 144. N. H. Col. II. 451, 488, 543. Conn. Col. II. 94, 147, 184.

DOUGLAS, WILLIAM (d. 1682). Judge (New London), 1667; Deputy (New London), May 1672, May 1676; Commissary for the Army, May 1676.
> Conn. Col. II. 63, 169, 274, 442.

DRAKE, SAMUEL (d. 1686). Deputy (Fairfield) to Conn. Leg., Oct. 1662.
> Conn. Col. I. 384.

DYER, JOHN (d. 1659). Served in Pequot War. (Residence, New London.)
> Mason's *Narrative*.

EAST, WILLIAM (d. 1681). Sergeant, Milford Train Band, prior to May 1654. Deputy (Milford), May 1666, Oct. 1666, May 1667, Oct. 1667, May 1668; Judge (Milford), 1688.
> N. H. Col. II. 90. Conn. Col. II. 31, 46, 58, 69, 83, 84.

EATON, SAMUEL (d. 1655). Assistant, N. H. Col., May 1654, May 1655; Judge (Southold town), May 1655.
> N. H. Col. II. 91, 140, 143.

EATON, THEOPHILUS (d. 1658). Chief Magistrate (New Haven), Oct. 1639, Oct. 1640, Oct. 1641, Oct. 1642; Governor, N. H. Col., Oct. 1643, Oct. 1646, May 1653, May 1654, May 1655, May 1656, May 1657; Commissioner to United Colonies, Apr. 1643, July 1643, Oct. 1643, Oct. 1646, May 1653, July 1654, May 1655, May 1656, May 1657. (He was Governor from 1643 until his death, Jan. 1658.)
> N. H. Col. I. 21, 44, 58, 78, 87, 96, 112, 117, 275. II. 1, 91, 111, 140, 168, 213.

CIVIL, MILITARY, AND ECCLESIASTICAL 17

EDWARDS, JOHN (d. 1664). Deputy (Wethersfield) to Conn. Leg., Apr. 1643.
Conn. Col. I. 84.

EELLS, SAMUEL (d. 1709). Sergeant, Milford Train Band, May 1669; Lieut., New Haven County Troop, May 1676; Lieut., Milford Train Band, Oct. 1676; Deputy (Milford), May 1677. (Removed to Hingham, Mass.)
Conn. Col. II. 107, 292, 300, 443.

EGGLESTON, JAMES (d. 1679). Granted 50 acres for service in Pequot War, Oct. 1671. (Residence, Windsor.)
Conn. Col. II. 162.

ELCOCK, ANTHONY (d. 1672). Second Drummer, N. H. Col. Troop, June 1654.
N. H. Col. II. 108.

ELDRED, SAMUEL (d. after 1697). Constable (Wickford), Oct. 1670, May 1671. Granted 20 nobles for his service and suffering (imprisoned by R. I. authorities, 1670).
Conn. Col. II. 138, 157, 241.

ELLIOT, JOSEPH (REV.) (d. 1694). Harvard College, 1658. Minister at Guilford, 1664–1694.

ELMER, EDWARD (d. 1676). Served in Pequot War. Lot in Soldiers' Field, Hartford.

ELY, NATHANIEL (d. 1675). Deputy (Norwalk) to Conn. Leg., Feb. 1657.
Conn. Col. I. 288.

EVANCE, JOHN. Judge (New Haven), Oct. 1643, Mar. 1644, Oct. 1644, Mar. 1645, Oct. 1645. (Returned to England.)
N. H. Col. I. 119, 125, 148, 156, 171.

FAIRCHILD, THOMAS (d. 1670). Deputy (Stratford) to Conn. Leg., Apr. 1646, Sept. 1654, May 1655, Oct. 1655, Oct. 1658, May 1659, Oct. 1659, May 1660, May 1664, Oct. 1664, Oct. 1665, May 1666, Oct. 1666, May 1667; Judge (Stratford), May 1664 to 1670 incl.; War Committee for Stratford, Oct. 1654.
Conn. Col. I. 138, 264, 274, 278, 323, 334, 340, 347, 425, 426, 431. II. 24, 31, 32, 47, 58, 63, 84, 106, 131.

FARNUM, HENRY (d. 1700). Deputy (Killingworth), May 1670, Oct. 1670.
Conn. Col. II. 126, 136.

FENN, BENJAMIN (d. 1672). Deputy (Milford) to N. H. Leg., May 1653; Assistant, N. H. Col., May 1654, May 1655, May 1656, May 1657, May 1658, May 1661, May 1662, May 1663, May 1664;

Commissioner to United Colonies, May 1661, May 1662, May 1663; Assistant (provisional appointment, Conn. Col.), Oct. 1664; Assistant, Conn. Col., May 1665 to 1672 incl. Granted 250 acres, May 1670.
N. H. Col. II. 2, 91, 140, 168, 213, 231, 402, 451, 488, 543. Conn. Col. I. 437. II. 13, 30, 58, 82, 104, 126, 133, 146, 169.

FENWICK, GEORGE (d. 1657). Assistant, Conn. Col., Apr. 1644, Apr. 1645, May 1647, May 1648; Commissioner for United Colonies, July 1643, Apr. 1644, July 1645. (Returned to England.)
Conn. Col. I. 90 (footnote), 103, 104, 124, 128, 149, 163.

FERMAN, ROBERT (d. 1671). Judge (Oyster Bay), May 1664.
Conn. Col. I. 428.

FERRIS, PETER (d. 1706). Deputy (Stamford), Oct. 1667.
Conn. Col. II. 70.

FIELD, ZACHARY (d. 1666). Served in Pequot War. (Removed to Hadley.) Lot in Soldiers' Field, Hartford.

FINCH, DANIEL (d. 1667). Constable (Wethersfield), Apr. 1636. (Removed to Stamford and Fairfield.)
Conn. Col. I. 1.

FITCH, JAMES (REV.) (d. 1702). Minister at Saybrook, 1646–1660; at Norwich, 1660–1702. Granted 100 acres, Oct. 1666; preacher of Election Sermon, May 1674; Chaplain to Army, May and July 1676.
Conn. Col. II. 49, 222, 279, 463.

FITCH, JOSEPH (d. 1727). Deputy (Hartford) to Conn. Leg., May 1662, Oct. 1662, May 1663, Oct. 1663, May 1664, Oct. 1664, May 1665, Oct. 1665, May 1666, Oct. 1666, May 1667, Oct. 1667, May 1668, Oct. 1668, May 1676; Militia Committee, July 1666; Commander of Hartford County Dragoons, Dec. 1675. (Removed to Windsor.)
Conn. Col. I. 378, 384, 399, 409, 425, 431. II. 13, 23, 31, 44, 46, 58, 69, 82, 93, 274, 390.

FITCH, SAMUEL (d. *c*. 1656). Deputy (Hartford) to Conn. Leg., May 1654, Sept. 1654, Oct. 1655.
Conn. Col. I. 256, 264, 278.

FITCH, THOMAS (d. 1704). Clerk, Norwalk Train Band, Feb. 1657; Ensign of same, May 1665; Capt., Fairfield County Troop, Aug. 1673, Feb. 1676. Deputy (Norwalk), May 1673; Judge (Norwalk), 1669 to 1677 incl.
Conn. Col. I. 290. II. 14, 106, 131, 152, 170, 192, 193, 206, 221, 250, 276, 304, 409.

FLETCHER, JOHN (d. 1662). Deputy (Milford) to N. H. Leg., May 1659, May 1661.
N. H. Col. II. 297, 403.

FOOTE, NATHANIEL (d. 1644). Deputy (Wethersfield) to Conn. Leg., Sept. 1641, Nov. 1641, Apr. 1644.
Conn. Col. I. 67, 69, 103.

Civil, Military, and Ecclesiastical

FOOTE, ROBERT (d. 1681). Lieut., Branford Train Band, May 1677.
Conn. Col. II. 304.

FORD, THOMAS (d. 1676). Deputy (Windsor) to Conn. Leg., Mar. 1638, Apr. 1638, Apr. 1639, Apr. 1640, Apr. 1641, Apr. 1644, May 1654.
Conn. Col. I. 13, 17, 27, 46, 64, 103, 256.

FOWLER, JOHN (d. 1676). Deputy (Guilford) to N. H. Leg., May 1661, Jan. 1664, May 1664; to Conn. Leg., Apr. 1665, May 1665, May 1666, Oct. 1666, May 1667, Oct. 1667, May 1668, Oct. 1668, May 1669, Oct. 1670, Oct. 1671, May 1672, Oct. 1672, May 1673, Oct. 1673, Oct. 1674, May 1675, Oct. 1675; Judge (Guilford), Oct. 1670. Sergeant, Guilford Train Band, July 1665. Called Deacon, Oct. 1668; granted 100 acres, May 1673.
N. H. Col. II. 403, 513, 544. Conn. Col. I. 439. II. 14, 22, 31, 47, 58, 70, 83, 94, 105, 136, 140, 160, 169, 184, 192, 200, 209, 236, 249, 265.

FOWLER, WILLIAM (d. 1661). Assistant, N. H. Col., Oct. 1643, Oct. 1646, May 1653; Deputy (Milford) to N. H. Leg., May 1657.
N. H. Col. I. 112, 275. II. 1, 213.

FOWLER, WILLIAM (d. 1683). Sergeant, New Haven Train Band, May 1647; Sergeant, Artillery Co., May 1648. Lieut., Milford Train Band, May 1666; Capt. of same, Oct. 1676; Deputy (Milford), Oct. 1669, May 1670, Oct. 1671, Oct. 1672, May 1673, Oct. 1673, May 1674, May 1675, May 1676, May 1677, Oct. 1677; War Committee, Aug. 1673; member of War Council, Nov. 1673.
N. H. Col. I. 313, 382. Conn. Col. II. 32, 115, 127, 160, 184, 192, 204, 209, 219, 221, 249, 274, 292, 300, 318.

FOWLES, RICHARD (d. *c.* 1685). Deputy (Greenwich) to Conn. Leg., Oct. 1665; Deputy (Hastings), Oct. 1668, May 1669. (Residence, Rye.)
Conn. Col. II. 24, 94, 106.

FUGILL, THOMAS. Judge (New Haven), Oct. 1639; Secretary, N. H. Col., Oct. 1643. (Returned to England.)
N. H. Col. I. 20, 112.

FYLER, WALTER (d. 1683). Deputy (Windsor) to Conn. Leg., Oct. 1661, May 1663, Oct. 1663; called Sergeant, Oct. 1642; first called Lieut., Oct. 1661. Granted 150 acres, May 1673.
Conn. Col. I. 76, 372, 399, 409. II. 194.

GALLUP, JOHN (d. 1675). Deputy (Stonington) to Conn. Leg., Oct. 1665, May 1667. Indian Overseer, May 1666. Granted 100 acres, May 1666; granted another 100 acres, Oct. 1671 for Pequot War service. (Capt., killed in King Philip's War.)
Conn. Col. II. 24, 36, 39, 59, 162.

GARDINER, LION (d. 1663). Lieut., in command of Fort at Saybrook, Pequot War.
<small>Gardiner's *Relation of the Pequot Wars*.</small>

GATES, GEORGE (d. 1724). Deputy (Haddam), Oct. 1668, May 1669, Oct. 1669, May 1670, Oct. 1670, May 1671, Oct. 1671, May 1672, Oct. 1672, May 1673, Oct. 1673, Oct. 1674, May 1675, Oct. 1675, May 1676, Oct. 1676, May 1677.
<small>Conn. Col. II. 94, 105, 116, 127, 136, 147, 159, 169, 184, 192, 209, 236, 249, 265, 274, 286, 300.</small>

GAYLORD, WILLIAM (d. 1673). Deputy (Windsor) to Conn. Leg., Apr. 1639, Sept. 1639, Jan. 1640, Apr. 1640, Feb. 1641, Apr. 1641, Nov. 1641, Apr. 1642, Aug. 1642, Mar. 1643, Apr. 1643, Sept. 1643, Apr. 1644, Sept. 1644, Apr. 1645, Sept. 1645, Apr. 1646, Sept. 1647, May 1649, Sept. 1649, May 1650, May 1651, May 1652, Sept. 1652, May 1653, Sept. 1653, Sept. 1654, May 1655, May 1656, Oct. 1656, May 1657, Oct. 1657, May 1658, Oct. 1658, May 1659, Oct. 1659, May 1660, Oct. 1660, May 1661, Oct. 1661, May 1662, May 1664.
<small>Conn. Col. I. 27, 34, 41, 46, 58, 64, 69, 71, 73, 82, 84, 93, 103, 111, 124, 130, 138, 157, 185, 195, 207, 218, 231, 235, 240, 246, 264, 274, 280, 282, 297, 306, 315, 323, 334, 340, 347, 353, 365, 372, 378, 425.</small>

GIBBARD, WILLIAM (d. 1663). Deputy (New Haven) to N. H. Leg., May 1652, May 1653, May 1654, May 1655, May 1656, May 1657, May 1658; Secretary, N. H. Col., May 1658, May 1659, May 1660; Assistant, N. H. Col., May 1661 (declined), May 1662; Judge (New Haven), Mar. 1645, Oct. 1645, Oct. 1646, Oct. 1647, May 1648, May 1649, May 1650, May 1651, May 1652, May 1653, May 1654, May 1655, May 1656, May 1657, May 1658, May 1659, May 1660, Oct. 1661.
<small>N. H. Col. I. 156, 171, 274, 354, 381, 456. II. 2, 92, 141, 169, 213, 231, 297, 360, 402, 451. N. H. Town I. 21, 72, 127, 180, 212, 240, 277, 313, 353, 402, 453, 489.</small>

GIBBS, JOHN (d. 1690). Deputy (Wethersfield) to Conn. Leg., Mar. 1638. Judge (New Haven), Oct. 1646, Oct. 1647.
<small>Conn. Col. I. 13. N. H. Col. I. 274, 354.</small>

GILBERT, JOHN (d. 1690). Accompanied Capt. Pynchon from Springfield to Fort Albany, July 1666; granted 200 acres, Oct. 1669. (Called Corporal; residence, Hartford.) Deputy (Haddam), Oct. 1673; Deputy (Stonington), Oct. 1675.
<small>Conn. Col. II. 43, 123, 209, 265.</small>

GILBERT, JONATHAN (d. 1682). Indian Interpreter, Conn. Leg., Apr. 1646; Marshal, Conn. Col., May 1662, May 1663, May 1664, and referred to as Marshal, Oct. 1668; Cornet of Troop of Horse, Oct. 1668; Deputy (Hartford), May 1677, Oct. 1677.
<small>Conn. Col. I. 139, 382, 401, 430. II. 101, 300, 318.</small>

CIVIL, MILITARY, AND ECCLESIASTICAL 21

GILBERT, MATTHEW (d. 1680). Judge (New Haven), Oct. 1639, Oct. 1640, May 1641, Oct. 1641, Apr. 1642, Oct. 1642, Apr. 1643; Assistant, N. H. Col., May 1658, May 1659, May 1660, May 1664; Dep. Governor, N. H. Col., May 1661, May 1662, May 1663. Assistant (provisional appointment, Conn. Col.), Oct. 1664; Assistant, 1677; Judge (New Haven), May 1665 to 1671 incl.
N. H. Col. I. 21, 44, 51, 58, 69, 78, 85. II. 231, 297, 359, 402, 451, 488, 543. Conn. Col. I. 437. II. 18, 32, 63, 84, 106, 131, 152, 300.

GILDERSLEEVE, RICHARD. Deputy (Stamford) to N. H. Leg., Apr. 1643, Oct. 1643. Judge (Hempstead), May 1664.
N. H. Col. I. 85, 112. Conn. Col. I. 428.

GILLETT, JEREMY, SR. (d. 1708). Granted 50 acres, May 1674. (Residence, Simsbury.)
Conn. Col. II. 230.

GILLETT, NATHAN (d. after 1688). Granted 50 acres, Oct. 1671 (for Pequot War service). (Residence, Windsor and Simsbury.)
Conn. Col. II. 161.

GISHOP, EDWARD, see JESSUP.

GLOVER, CHARLES. Acting Lieut., Southold Train Band, May 1654; Lieut. of same, May 1661.
N. H. Col. II. 97, 407.

GOLD, NATHAN (d. 1694). First called Ensign, May 1656; Lieut., Fairfield Train Band, May 1657; Judge (Fairfield), May 1656, May 1657; Assistant, Conn. Col., May 1657, May 1659 to 1677 incl.; Patentee, Royal Charter, 1662. Chief Military Officer, Fairfield County, June 1672; Major, Fairfield County, Aug. 1673; member of War Council, Nov. 1673, July 1675, May 1676. Granted 300 acres, Oct. 1667.
Conn. Col. I. 281, 297, 299, 300, 334, 347, 364, 378, 384, 398, 425. II. 4, 13, 30, 57, 77, 82, 104, 126, 146, 169, 183, 191, 206, 219, 221, 248, 261, 274, 284, 300.

GOODMAN, RICHARD (d. 1676). Served in Pequot War. (Removed to Hadley.) Lot in Soldiers' Field, Hartford.

GOODRICH, WILLIAM (d. 1676). Served in Pequot War; Ensign, Wethersfield Train Band, May 1665. Deputy (Wethersfield) to Conn. Leg., May 1660, Oct. 1660, May 1662, Oct. 1665, May 1666, Oct. 1666.
Conn. Col. I. 347, 354, 379. II. 17, 24, 31, 47.

GOODYEAR, STEPHEN (d. 1658). Judge (New Haven), May 1641; Dep. Magistrate (New Haven), Oct. 1641, Oct. 1642; Dep. Governor, N. H. Col., Oct. 1643, Oct. 1646, May 1653, May 1654, May 1655, May 1656, May 1657; Commissioner for United Colonies, Oct. 1646. (He was Dep. Governor from 1643 to the end of the 1657 term.)
N. H. Col. I. 51, 58, 78, 112, 275. II. 1, 91, 140, 168, 213.

GOSMER, JOHN (d. 1660–1). Assistant, Conn. Col., May 1647, May 1648, May 1649, May 1650, May 1655, May 1657, May 1658. (Residence, Southampton, L. I.)
Conn. Col. I. 149, 163, 185, 207, 274, 297, 314.

GOULD, THOMAS (d. 1693). Judge (Wickford), Oct. 1670, May 1673.
Conn. Col. II. 138, 198.

GRANT, MATTHEW (d. 1681). Granted 100 acres, May 1673. (Residence, Windsor.)
Conn. Col. II. 198.

GRAVES, GEORGE (d. 1692). Deputy (Hartford) to Conn. Leg., Feb. 1657, Oct. 1657, May 1658, Oct. 1658. Sealer of Measures, Oct. 1670; in King Philip's War, Sept. 1675; Marshal, 1676, 1677.
Conn. Col. I. 288, 306, 315, 323. II. 141, 275, 309, 360.

GRAVES, JOHN (d. 1695). Ensign, Guilford Train Band, Oct. 1667; Deputy (Guilford), May 1670, May 1671, Oct. 1671, May 1672, Oct. 1672, May 1673, May 1674, May 1675, Oct. 1676, Oct. 1677. Granted 100 acres, May 1673.
Conn. Col. II. 74, 126, 147, 160, 169, 184, 192, 200, 221, 249, 286, 318.

GRAVES, JOHN. Deputy (Middletown), Oct. 1676, then called Sergeant.
Conn. Col. II. 287.

GRAY, HENRY (d. 1658). Deputy (Fairfield) to Conn. Leg., Apr. 1643, Oct. 1656, Feb. 1657.
Conn. Col. I. 84, 282, 288.

GREEN, JOHN. Deputy (Stamford), Oct. 1668, May 1669, Oct. 1669, May 1670, May 1671, Oct. 1671, May 1673, Oct. 1673, Oct. 1674.
Conn. Col. II. 95, 106, 116, 126, 147, 160, 192, 209, 236.

GREGORY, JOHN (d. 1689). Deputy (Norwalk) to Conn. Leg., Oct. 1659, Oct. 1662, May 1663, May 1665, Oct. 1667, May 1668, May 1669, Oct. 1669, Oct. 1670, Oct. 1671, May 1672, May 1674, Oct. 1675, Oct. 1677.
Conn. Col. I. 340, 384, 399. II. 14, 70, 83, 105, 116, 136, 159, 170, 221, 265, 318.

GREGSON, THOMAS (d. 1646). Judge (New Haven), Oct. 1640, May 1641, Oct. 1641, Apr. 1642, Oct. 1642, Apr. 1643; Assistant, N. H. Col., Oct. 1643, Oct. 1646; Commissioner for United Colonies, Apr. 1643, July 1643, Oct. 1643; Colonial Agent to Parliament, Nov. 1644.
N. H. Col. I. 44, 51, 58, 69, 78, 85, 87, 96, 112, 117, 149, 211, 275.

GRIDLEY, THOMAS (d. 1655). Grant of 50 acres to his heirs, Oct. 1671 (for Pequot War service). (Residence, Hartford.)
Conn. Col. II. 161.

CIVIL, MILITARY, AND ECCLESIASTICAL 23

GRIFFIN, JOHN (d. 1681). Deputy for Simsbury, Oct. 1670, May 1671, May 1672, Oct. 1673, May 1674; Second Officer, Simsbury Train Band, Aug. 1673; Sergeant (Commanding Officer) of same, July 1675.
Conn. Col. II. 136, 147, 169, 208, 209, 221, 332.

GRISWOLD, EDWARD (d. 1691). Deputy (Windsor) to Conn. Leg., May 1656, May 1658, Oct. 1658, May 1659, Oct. 1659, May 1660, Oct. 1660, May 1662, Oct. 1662; Deputy (Killingworth), May 1667, May 1668, Oct. 1668, May 1669, Oct. 1669, May 1670, Oct. 1670, Oct. 1671, May 1672, Oct. 1672, May 1673, Oct. 1673, May 1674, Oct. 1674, May 1675, Oct. 1675, May 1676, Oct. 1676, May 1677, Oct. 1677; Judge (Killingworth), 1667, 1668, 1669, 1670, 1671, 1672, 1673, 1674, 1675, 1676, 1677. Granted 200 acres, Oct. 1674.
Conn. Col. I. 281, 315, 323, 334, 340, 347, 353, 378, 384. II. 58, 63, 82, 84, 94, 105, 106, 116, 126, 131, 136, 152, 159, 169, 170, 184, 192, 193, 209, 221, 236, 240, 250, 265, 274, 275, 286, 300, 304, 318.

GRISWOLD, FRANCIS (d. 1671). Deputy (Norwich) to Conn. Leg., Oct. 1664, May 1665, Oct. 1665, May 1666, Oct. 1666, May 1667, Oct. 1667, May 1668, Oct. 1668, May 1669, May 1671; Committee on Stonington Indians, Oct. 1666, then called Lieut.; granted 100 acres, May 1668.
Conn. Col. I. 431. II. 14, 24, 31, 47, 56, 59, 70, 83, 91, 94, 106, 147.

GRISWOLD, MATTHEW (d. 1699). Deputy (Saybrook) to Conn. Leg., May 1649, May 1650, May 1654, May 1660; Deputy (Lyme), Oct. 1667, May 1668, Oct. 1668, May 1669, May 1671, Oct. 1671, May 1672, Oct. 1672, May 1673, Oct. 1673, May 1674, May 1677, Oct. 1677; Judge (Lyme), 1669, 1670; Commissioner to R. I., Oct. 1668; Lieut., Lyme Train Band, May 1677.
Conn. Col. I. 185, 207, 256, 347. II. 70, 83, 94, 103, 106, 131, 147, 159, 170, 184, 192, 209, 221, 300, 317, 318.

GROVES, PHILIP (d. 1676). Deputy (Stratford) to Conn. Leg., Apr. 1642, May 1648, May 1651, May 1653, May 1654, May 1655, Oct. 1655, Feb. 1657, May 1660, Oct. 1660, May 1661, Oct. 1661, Oct. 1662, May 1663, Oct. 1663, May 1665; Judge (Stratford), May 1654, May 1655, May 1656; War Committee for Stratford, May 1653, Oct. 1654.
Conn. Col. I. 71, 163, 218, 240, 243, 256, 257, 264, 274, 278, 281, 288, 347, 354, 365, 372, 384, 399, 410. II. 13.

GUNN, JASPER (d. 1671). Deputy (Milford) to N. H. Leg., May 1663.
N. H. Col. II. 477.

HALE, SAMUEL (d. 1691). Served in Pequot War. Deputy (Norwalk) to Conn. Leg., Oct. 1656, Feb. 1657, Oct. 1657, May 1660, Oct. 1660; Deputy (Wethersfield), May 1665. Granted 60 acres "upon the same tearmes with the Pequot soldiers," May 1671.
Conn. Col. I. 283, 288, 306, 347, 354. II. 13, 151.

HALE, THOMAS (d. 1679). Granted 50 acres for Pequot War service, Oct. 1671. (Residence, Hartford, Norwalk, etc.)
Conn. Col. II. 162.

HALL, FRANCIS (d. 1690). Deputy (Stratford) to Conn. Leg., May 1661, May 1676, Oct. 1677.
Conn. Col. I. 365. II. 274, 318.

HALL, JOHN (d. 1676). Served in Pequot War. (Removed to Wallingford.)
Conn. Col. IV. 276.

HALL, JOHN, JR. (d. 1695). Deputy (Middletown) to Conn. Leg., May 1653.
Conn. Col. I. 240.

HALLETT, WILLIAM. Judge (Flushing), May 1664.
Conn. Col. I. 428.

HALSEY, THOMAS, SR. (d. 1678). Deputy (Southampton, L. I.) to Conn. Leg., May 1664.
Conn. Col. I. 425.

HAMLIN, GILES (d. 1689). Deputy (Middletown), May 1666, Oct. 1666, May 1667, Oct. 1667, May 1668, Oct. 1668, Oct. 1670, May 1671, Oct. 1671, May 1673, Oct. 1673, May 1674, May 1675; Judge (Middletown), 1666, 1667, 1668, 1669, 1670, (Middletown and Haddam), 1671, 1672, 1673, 1674, 1675, 1676, 1677; Committee on Indians, May 1668; War Committee, Aug. 1673.
Conn. Col. II. 31, 32, 47, 58, 63, 70, 82, 84, 88, 94, 106, 131, 136, 147, 152, 159, 170, 192, 204, 209, 221, 249, 250, 275, 304.

HANFORD, THOMAS (REV.) (d. 1693). Minister at Norwalk, 1654–1693. Granted 200 acres, Oct. 1674.
Conn. Col. II. 241.

HARRIS, DANIEL (d. 1701). Capt., Middletown Train Band, May 1677.
Conn. Col. II. 304.

HARRIS, GABRIEL (d. 1684). Ensign, New London Train Band, May 1665.
Conn. Col. II. 17.

HARRISON, THOMAS (d. 1704). Deputy (Branford), May 1677, Oct. 1677; Ensign, Branford Train Band, May 1677 (erroneously called Harris).
Conn. Col. II. 300, 304, 318.

HART, JOHN (d. 1666). Deputy (Farmington) to Conn. Leg., May 1659, Oct. 1659.
Conn. Col. I. 334, 340.

CIVIL, MILITARY, AND ECCLESIASTICAL 25

HART, STEPHEN (d. 1683). Deputy (Farmington) to Conn. Leg., May 1647, May 1648, May 1649, Sept. 1649, May 1650, Sept. 1650, May 1651, Sept. 1651, Sept. 1652, May 1653, Sept. 1653, Sept. 1654, May 1655, May 1660; War Committee for Farmington, May 1653. Granted 150 acres, May 1673 (for service in Pequot War).
Conn. Col. I. 149, 163, 185, 195, 207, 211, 218, 224, 235, 240, 243, 246, 264, 274, 347. II. 193.

HARVEY, EDMUND (d. 1648). Deputy (Fairfield) to Conn. Leg., May 1647.
Conn. Col. I. 149.

HARVEY, JOSIAH (d. 1698). Chirurgeon to Army, Oct. 1675. (Residence, Fairfield.)
Conn. Col. II. 268.

HAWLEY, JOSEPH (d. 1690). Deputy (Stratford) to Conn. Leg., May 1658, Oct. 1665, Oct. 1667, May 1668, Oct. 1668, May 1669, Oct. 1669, May 1670, Oct. 1670, May 1671, Oct. 1671, Oct. 1673, May 1674, Oct. 1674, Oct. 1675, May 1677.
Conn. Col. I. 315. II. 24, 70, 83, 94, 105, 116, 127, 136, 147, 159, 209, 221, 236, 265, 300.

HAYDEN, WILLIAM (d. 1669). Deputy (Killingworth), Oct. 1667. Grant of 50 acres to his heirs, Oct. 1671 (for Pequot War service). (Residence, Hartford, Windsor, Killingworth.)
Conn. Col. II. 70, 161.

HAYNES, JOHN (d. 1653). Commissioner to Saybrook, Pequot War, June 1637; Assistant, Conn. Col., Nov. 1637, Feb. 1638, Mar. 1638, Apr. 1638, Apr. 1642, May 1648; Governor, Conn. Col., Apr. 1639, Apr. 1641, Apr. 1643, Apr. 1645, May 1647, May 1649, May 1651, May 1653; Dep. Governor, Conn. Col., Apr. 1640, Apr. 1644, Apr. 1646, May 1650, May 1652; Commissioner for United Colonies, Mar. 1643, Apr. 1646.
Conn. Col. I. 10, 11, 13, 17, 27, 46, 64, 71, 82, 84, 103, 124, 137, 139, 149, 163, 185, 207, 218, 230, 240.

HAYNES, JOSEPH (REV.) (d. 1679). Harvard College, 1658. Minister at Wethersfield, 1663–1664; at Hartford, 1664–1679.

HEDGE, MR. An unidentified soldier of the Pequot War, a gentleman of Northamptonshire. Perhaps William Hedge of Yarmouth; or Tristram Hedges who was at Southampton, L. I., 1644, owned land in Huntington, L. I., and was of Boston, 1657.

HICKS, JOHN (d. 1672). Judge (Hempstead), May 1664.
Conn. Col. I. 428.

HIGGINSON, JOHN (REV.) (d. 1708). Chaplain at Saybrook. Fort, Pequot War. Minister at Guilford, 1641–1659; at Salem, Mass., 1660–1708.

HILL, CHARLES (d. 1684). Deputy (New London), Oct. 1675.
Conn. Col. II. 265.

HILL, WILLIAM (d. 1649). Deputy (Windsor) to Conn. Leg., Aug. 1639, Sept. 1639, Jan. 1640, Feb. 1641, Sept. 1641, Nov. 1641, Apr. 1642, Aug. 1642, Mar. 1643, Sept. 1643, Apr. 1644, Sept. 1644.
Conn. Col. I. 29, 34, 41, 58, 67, 69, 71, 73, 82, 93, 103, 111.

HILL, WILLIAM (d. 1684). Deputy (Fairfield) to Conn. Leg., Sept. 1651, May 1652, Oct. 1652, May 1653, May 1654, Sept. 1654, May 1655, Oct. 1655, Oct. 1658, Oct. 1659, Oct. 1661, Oct. 1665, Oct. 1666, May 1667, Oct. 1667, May 1668, Oct. 1668, May 1669, May 1671; War Committee for Fairfield, May 1653; Judge (Fairfield), 1666 to 1677 incl.; Clerk of Fairfield County Court, May 1666. Granted 150 acres, Oct. 1672.
Conn. Col. I. 224, 231, 235, 240, 243, 256, 264, 274, 278, 323, 340, 372. II. 24, 31, 38, 46, 58, 63, 70, 83, 84, 94, 105, 106, 131, 147, 152, 170, 187, 193, 221, 250, 276, 304.

HILLS, JOHN (d. 1692). Granted 50 acres, Oct. 1671 (for Pequot War service). (Residence, Hartford.)
Conn. Col. II. 161.

HOLCOLM, JOSHUA (d. 1690). Deputy (Simsbury), May 1670, May 1671.
Conn. Col. II. 126, 147.

HOLLISTER, JOHN (d. 1665). Deputy (Wethersfield) to Conn. Leg., Sept. 1644, Apr. 1645, Sept. 1645, Dec. 1645, May 1650, Oct. 1653, May 1654, Sept. 1654, May 1655, Oct. 1656, Feb. 1657, Oct. 1657, May 1658, Oct. 1658, May 1659, Oct. 1661. First called Lieut., Apr. 1657; War Committee for Wethersfield, Oct. 1654.
Conn. Col. I. 111, 124, 130, 133, 207, 248, 256, 264, 274, 282, 288, 293, 306, 315, 323, 334, 372.

HOLLISTER, THOMAS (d. 1701). Mentioned as Lieut. at Wethersfield, May 1676; Lieut., Hartford County Troop, June 1676; Lieut., Oct. 1677.
Conn. Col. II. 319, 439, 458.

HOLLOWAY, JOHN (d. 1684). Granted 50 acres for service in Pequot War, May 1671. (Residence, Hartford.)
Conn. Col. II. 154.

HOLLY, JOHN (d. 1681). Judge (Stamford), May 1654, May 1655; Deputy (Stamford) to N. H. Leg., May 1663; Judge (Stamford, Greenwich, and Rye), 1667, 1668, 1670, 1671, 1672, 1673, 1674, 1675, 1676, 1677; Deputy (Stamford), Oct. 1670, (Greenwich), May 1673.
N. H. Col. II. 96, 148, 477. Conn. Col. II. 63, 84, 132, 136, 152, 170, 192, 193, 221, 250, 276, 304.

HOOKE, WILLIAM (REV.) (d. 1677). Minister at New Haven, 1644; returned to England, 1656.

Civil, Military, and Ecclesiastical 27

HOOKER, SAMUEL (REV.) (d. 1697). Harvard College, 1653. Minister at Farmington, 1661-1697. Commissioner to treat with New Haven Colony, Oct. 1662. Granted 250 acres, Oct. 1667; preacher of Election Sermon, May 1677.
Conn. Col. I. 388. II. 77, 307.

HOOKER, THOMAS (REV.) (d. 1647). Minister at Hartford, 1635-1647.

HOPKINS, EDWARD (d. 1657). Deputy (Hartford) to Conn. Leg., Mar. 1638, Apr. 1638; Assistant, Conn. Col., Apr. 1639, Apr. 1641, Apr. 1642, May 1655, May 1656; Secretary, Conn. Col., Apr. 1639; Governor, Conn. Col., Apr. 1640, Apr. 1644, Apr. 1646, May 1648, May 1650, May 1652, May 1654; Dep. Governor, Conn. Col., Apr. 1643, Apr. 1645, May 1647, May 1649, May 1651, May 1653; Commissioner for United Colonies, Mar. 1643, July 1643, Apr. 1644, July 1645, Apr. 1646, Jan. 1647, May 1648, May 1649, May 1651. (Returned to England.)
Conn. Col. I. 13, 17, 27, 46, 64, 71, 82, 84, 90, 103, 104, 124, 128, 137, 139, 147, 149, 163, 164, 185, 187, 207, 218, 222, 230, 240, 256, 274, 280.

HOPKINS, WILLIAM. Assistant, Conn. Col., Apr. 1641, Apr. 1642.
Conn. Col. I. 64, 71.

HORTON, BARNABAS (d. 1680). Deputy (Southold) to N. H. Leg., May 1654, May 1656, May 1658, May 1659, May 1661; Judge (Southold), May 1654, May 1656, May 1658, May 1659, May 1663, May 1664.
N. H. Col. II. 92, 95, 169, 172, 232, 236, 298, 304, 403. Conn. Col. I. 402, 428.

HORTON, JOSEPH (d. c. 1696). Lieut., Rye Train Band, May 1667; Deputy (Rye), May 1672; Commissioner, N. Y. Boundary, Oct. 1674.
Conn. Col. II. 63, 170, 242.

HOSFORD, WILLIAM. Deputy (Windsor) to Conn. Leg., May 1637, Sept. 1652. (Returned to England.)
Conn. Col. I. 9, 235.

HOWELL, EDWARD (d. 1656). Assistant, Conn. Col., May 1647, May 1648, May 1649, May 1650, May 1651, May 1652, May 1653.
Conn. Col. I. 149, 163, 185, 207, 218, 231, 240.

HOWELL, JOHN (d. 1696). Deputy (Southampton) to Conn. Leg., Oct. 1662; Assistant, Conn. Col., May 1664. Judge (Southampton), May 1674, called Captain.
Conn. Col. I. 384, 425. II. 229.

HOWKINS, ANTHONY (d. 1674). Deputy (Farmington) to Conn. Leg., Oct. 1657, May 1658, May 1660, Oct. 1660, May 1661, Oct. 1661, May 1662, Oct. 1662, May 1663, Oct. 1663, May 1664, Oct. 1664, May 1665, Oct. 1665, Oct. 1666, May 1667, Oct. 1667; Patentee,

Royal Charter, 1662; Assistant, 1668-1674; Judge (Farmington), 1663, 1664, 1666, 1667; Militia Committee, July 1666; member of War Council, Nov. 1673; granted 50 acres in addition to former 200, Oct. 1668, and 50 acres more, May 1671.
   Conn. Col. I. 306, 315, 347, 354, 365, 372, 379, 384, 399, 401, 410, 425, 426, 431. II. 4, 14, 24, 31, 44, 46, 58, 63, 70, 82, 100, 104, 126, 146, 151, 169, 191, 219.

HOWKINS, JOHN (d. 1676). Mentioned as Sergeant at Farmington, May 1676.
   Conn. Col. II. 439.

HOYT, NICHOLAS. Deputy (Norwalk), Oct. 1672. (Probably an error in the record for Walter, see below.)
   Conn. Col. II. 184.

HOYT, WALTER (d. 1699). Deputy (Norwalk) to Conn. Leg., Oct. 1658, Oct. 1659, Oct. 1661, May 1667, Oct. 1667, Oct. 1668, May 1670, May 1671, Oct. 1673, Oct. 1674, May 1676; Sergeant, Norwalk Train Band, May 1659.
   Conn. Col. I. 323, 336, 340, 372. II. 59, 70, 94, 127, 147, 209, 236, 274.

HUBBARD, GEORGE (d. 1683). Deputy (Wethersfield) to Conn. Leg., Mar. 1638, Apr. 1638, Apr. 1639, Aug. 1639, Sept. 1639, Apr. 1640, Feb. 1641, Apr. 1641, Apr. 1642, Aug. 1642. Deputy (Guilford) to N. H. Leg., May 1655, May 1657, May 1658, May 1659, Aug. 1661, May 1662; Deputy (Guilford) to Conn. Leg., Oct. 1665, Oct. 1666; Judge (Guilford), May 1665, 1666, 1667, Oct. 1670.
   Conn. Col. I. 13, 17, 27, 29, 34, 46, 58, 64, 71, 73. II. 18, 24, 32, 47, 63, 140. N. H. Col. II. 141, 214, 232, 297, 418, 451.

HUBBARD, JAMES (d. after 1676). Judge (Gravesend), May 1664.
   Conn. Col. I. 429.

HUDSON, WILLIAM (CAPT.) Judge (Wickford), Oct. 1670, May 1671.
   Conn. Col. II. 138, 157.

HUET, EPHRAIM (REV.) (d. 1644). Minister at Windsor, 1639-1644.

HULL, CORNELIUS (d. 1695). Deputy (Fairfield) to Conn. Leg., Feb. 1657, May 1658, May 1659, May 1660, Oct. 1660, Oct. 1662, May 1663, Oct. 1664, May 1667, Oct. 1676, Oct. 1677; Lieut. of Maj. Treat's Life Guard, Feb. 1676; Lieut., Fairfield County Troop, May 1676. Granted 100 acres, Oct. 1677.
   Conn. Col. I. 288, 315, 334, 347, 354, 384, 399, 431. II. 58, 279, 287, 318, 327, 411.

HULL, GEORGE (d. 1659). Deputy (Windsor) to Conn. Leg., May 1637, Nov. 1637, Mar. 1638, Apr. 1638, Aug. 1639, Sept. 1639, Jan. 1640, Apr. 1640, Feb. 1641, Apr. 1641, Sept. 1641, Nov. 1641, Apr. 1642, Aug. 1642, Mar. 1643, Apr. 1643, Sept. 1643, Apr. 1644, Sept.

1644, Sept. 1645, Dec. 1645, Apr. 1646; Deputy (Fairfield), May 1649, May 1650, May 1651, Oct. 1655, May 1656; Judge (Fairfield), May 1654.
><small>Conn. Col. I. 9, 11, 13, 17, 29, 34, 41, 46, 58, 64, 67, 69, 71, 73, 82, 84, 93, 103, 111, 130, 133, 138, 185, 207, 218, 257, 278, 281.</small>

HULL, JOHN (d. 1711). Surgeon, King Philip's War, Oct. 1675 (name printed Hall), Feb. and May 1676.
><small>Conn. Col. II. 268, 286, 409, 455.</small>

HULL, JOSIAH, SR. (d. 1675). Deputy (Windsor) to Conn. Leg., May 1659, Oct. 1659, Oct. 1660, Oct. 1662. Lieut., Killingworth Train Band, Oct. 1666; Deputy (Killingworth), May 1667, May 1668, Oct. 1668, May 1669, Oct. 1669, Oct. 1671, May 1672, Oct. 1672, May 1673, Oct. 1673, May 1674; Judge (Killingworth), 1671.
><small>Conn. Col. I. 334, 340, 347, 384. II. 50, 59, 83, 94, 105, 116, 152, 159, 169, 184, 192, 209, 221.</small>

HUMPHREY, MICHAEL (d. c. 1695). Deputy (Simsbury), Oct. 1670.
><small>Conn. Col. II. 136.</small>

HUNT, THOMAS (d. 1694). Deputy (Westchester) to Conn. Leg., Oct. 1664.
><small>Conn. Col. I. 431.</small>

HUNTINGTON, CHRISTOPHER (d. 1691). Granted 100 acres, Oct. 1668. (Residence, Norwich.)
><small>Conn. Col. II. 96.</small>

HUNTINGTON, SIMON (d. 1706). Deputy (Norwich), May 1674, Oct. 1677.
><small>Conn. Col. II. 221, 318.</small>

HURD, JOHN (d. 1682). Deputy (Stratford) to Conn. Leg., May 1649, May 1656, Oct. 1656, Oct. 1657.
><small>Conn. Col. I. 185, 281, 283, 306.</small>

HURLBUT, THOMAS (d. 1689). Granted 120 acres, Oct. 1671 (for Pequot War service). Clerk, Wethersfield Train Band, June 1649.
><small>Conn. Col. I. 189. II. 161.</small>

HUTCHINSON, EDWARD (CAPT.). Judge (Wickford), Oct. 1670, May 1671.
><small>Conn. Col. II. 138, 157.</small>

INCE, JONATHAN (d. 1657?). Served in Pequot War. Lot in Soldiers' Field, Hartford.

JAGGER, JEREMY (d. 1658). His three sons granted 20 acres apiece for his service in Pequot War, May 1671. (Residence, Stamford.)
><small>Conn. Col. II. 150.</small>

JEFFREYS, THOMAS (d. 1661). Sergeant, New Haven Train Band,

Aug. 1642; Sergeant, Artillery Co., Mar. 1645; Sergeant with Lieut. Seeley against Ninigret, Oct. 1654.
N. H. Col. I. 76, 158. II. 120.

JENNINGS, NICHOLAS (d. 1673). Served in Pequot War. (Removed to Saybrook.) Lot in Soldiers' Field, Hartford.

JESSUP, EDWARD. (d. 1666). Judge (Westchester), Oct. 1663, May 1664.
Conn. Col. I. 412 (called Gishop), 426.

JESSUP, JOHN (d. after 1684). Deputy (Southampton) to Conn. Leg., May 1664.
Conn. Col. I. 425. Southampton T. R. II. 229.

JOHNSON, JOHN (d. 1681). Granted 50 acres, Oct. 1671 (for Pequot War service). (Residence, Guilford.)
Conn. Col. II. 161.

JOHNSON, WILLIAM (d. 1702). Sergeant, Guilford Train Band, July 1665. Deputy (Guilford) to Conn. Leg., Oct. 1665, May 1667, Oct. 1667, May 1668, Oct. 1668, May 1669, Oct. 1669, Oct. 1670, May 1671, May 1674, May 1676; Judge (Guilford), Oct. 1670; granted 100 acres, May 1673.
Conn. Col. II. 22, 24, 58, 70, 83, 94, 105, 116, 136, 140, 147, 200, 221, 274.

JONES, ELIPHALET (REV.) (d. 1731). Minister at Greenwich, 1669–1672; at Stamford, 1672; at Huntington, L. I., from 1673.

JONES, JOHN (REV.) (d. 1665). Minister at Concord, Mass., 1637–1644; at Fairfield, 1644–1665.

JONES, WILLIAM (d. 1706). Assistant, N. H. Col., May 1662, May 1663; Dep. Governor, N. H. Col., May 1664; Commissioner to United Colonies, May 1664; Commissioner to treat with Conn. Col., May 1664; Assistant (provisional appointment, Conn. Col.), Oct. 1664; Assistant, Conn. Col., May 1665 to 1677 incl.; Judge (New Haven), May 1665; Militia Committee, June 1672; member of War Council, Nov. 1673, July 1675, May 1676. Granted 300 acres, May 1671.
N. H. Col. II. 451, 488, 542, 543. Conn. Col. I. 437. II. 13, 18, 30, 57, 82, 104, 126, 146, 151, 169, 183, 191, 219, 221, 248, 261, 274, 284, 300.

JORDAN, THOMAS. Deputy (Guilford) to N. H. Leg., May 1653, May 1654; Commissioner to Mass. Col., June 1653, June 1654. (Returned to England.)
N. H. Col. II. 2, 5, 92, 101.

JUDD, THOMAS (d. 1688). Deputy (Farmington) to Conn. Leg., May 1647, May 1648, May 1649, Sept. 1650, Nov. 1650, Sept. 1651, Feb. 1657, Oct. 1658, Oct. 1659, May 1661, Oct. 1661, May 1662, Oct.

CIVIL, MILITARY, AND ECCLESIASTICAL 31

1662, May 1663, Oct. 1663, May 1666, Oct. 1668, Oct. 1670, May 1677, Oct. 1677; called Deacon, 1668.
Conn. Col. I. 149, 163, 185, 211, 213, 224, 288, 323, 340, 365, 372, 379, 384, 399, 410. II. 31, 94, 136, 300, 318.

JUDSON, JOSEPH (d. 1690). Deputy (Stratford) to Conn. Leg., Oct. 1658, May 1659, Oct. 1659, Oct. 1661, May 1662, Oct. 1662, May 1663, Oct. 1663, May 1664, May 1665, May 1666, Oct. 1666, May 1667. First called Ensign, Oct. 1663; Lieut., Stratford Train Band, June 1672; alternate Capt., Fairfield County Troop, May 1676.
Conn. Col. I. 323, 334, 340, 372, 379, 384, 399, 410, 425. II. 13, 31, 47, 58, 181, 279.

KELLOGG, DANIEL (d. 1688). Deputy (Norwalk), Oct. 1670, May 1672, Oct. 1674, Oct. 1675, May 1677.
Conn. Col. II. 136, 170, 236, 265, 300.

KELSEY, WILLIAM (d. *c.* 1680). Deputy (Killingworth), May 1671.
Conn. Col. II. 147.

KETCHUM, JOHN. Deputy (Setauket) to Conn. Leg., May 1664; Judge (Setauket), May 1664.
Conn. Col. I. 425, 428.

KILBOURN, JOHN (d. 1703). Sergeant, Wethersfield Train Band, May 1657. Deputy (Wethersfield) to Conn. Leg., Oct. 1660, May 1661, May 1662.
Conn. Col. I. 299, 354, 365, 379.

KIMBERLY, THOMAS (d. 1672). Corporal, New Haven Train Band, Aug. 1642. Marshal, N. H. Col., Oct. 1643, Oct. 1646, May 1653, May 1654, May 1655, May 1656, May 1657, May 1658, May 1659, May 1660, May 1661.
N. H. Col. I. 76, 112, 276. II. 1, 92, 140, 168, 213, 231, 297, 360, 403.

KITCHELL, ROBERT (d. 1672). Deputy (Guilford) to N. H. Leg., May 1656, May 1661, May 1662, May 1663, Oct. 1663; Judge (Guilford), May 1665, 1666, 1667. (Removed to Newark, N. J.)
N. H. Col. II. 169, 403, 451, 488, 500. Conn. Col. II. 18, 32, 63.

KITCHELL, SAMUEL (d. 1690). Ensign, Guilford Train Band, July 1665. (Removed to Newark, N. J.)
Conn. Col. II. 22.

KNAPP, TIMOTHY (d. after 1697). Deputy (Rye), Oct. 1670, Oct. 1676.
Conn. Col. II. 136, 287.

KNELL, NICHOLAS (d. 1675). Granted 50 acres, May 1668, and 50 acres more, May 1669. (Residence, Stratford.)
Conn. Col. II. 83, 113.

KNOWLES, ALEXANDER (d. 1663). Judge (Fairfield), May 1654, May 1661; Assistant, Conn. Col., May 1658; War Committee for Fairfield, Oct. 1654.
Conn. Col. I. 257, 264, 314, 366.

LAMBERTON, GEORGE (d. 1646). Deputy (New Haven) to N. H. Leg., Oct. 1643, Oct. 1645; Judge (New Haven), Mar. 1644.
N. H. Col. I. 111, 125, 173.

LANGTON, JOHN (d. 1689). Deputy (Farmington), Oct. 1668.
Conn. Col. II. 94.

LATHAM, CARY (d. 1685). Deputy (New London) to Conn. Leg., May 1664, May 1666, May 1667, Oct. 1667, May 1668, May 1670; Indian Overseer, May 1666.
Conn. Col. I. 425. II. 31, 39, 58, 70, 83, 127.

LATHROP, SAMUEL (d. 1700). Judge (New London), May 1649.
Conn. Col. I. 186.

LATTIMER, JOHN (d. 1662). Deputy (Wethersfield) to Conn. Leg., May 1654.
Conn. Col. I. 256.

LAW, RICHARD (d. 1687). Deputy (Stamford) to N. H. Leg., May 1653, May 1654, May 1655, May 1656, May 1657, May 1658, May 1659, May 1661, May 1662, May 1663, Oct. 1663, Jan. 1664, May 1664; Judge (Stamford), May 1653, May 1654, May 1655, May 1656, May 1657, May 1658, May 1660, May 1661, May 1662, May 1663. Assistant (provisional appointment, Conn. Col.), Oct. 1664; Judge (Stamford, Greenwich, and Rye), May 1665 to 1677 incl.; Deputy (Stamford) to Conn. Leg., Oct. 1665, Oct. 1666, Oct. 1669, May 1672.
N. H. Col. II. 2, 92, 96, 141, 147, 169, 172, 214, 215, 232, 235, 297, 369, 403, 405, 451, 453, 477, 489, 500, 513, 544. Conn. Col. I. 437. II. 14, 24, 31, 47, 63, 84, 106, 116, 131, 152, 170, 193, 221, 250, 276, 304.

LAY, EDWARD (d. 1692). Served in Pequot War. (Removed to Portsmouth, R. I.)
Shepard.

LAY, ROBERT. Deputy (Saybrook), Oct. 1666.
Conn. Col. II. 47.

LEE, THOMAS (d. 1704). Deputy (Lyme), Oct. 1676.
Conn. Col. II. 286.

LEEK, PHILIP (d. 1676). Corporal, New Haven Train Band, Mar. 1645 (resigned May 1652).
N. H. Col. I. 160. N. H. Town I. 127.

LEETE, ANDREW (d. 1702). Deputy (Guilford), Oct. 1675, May 1676, Oct. 1676, May 1677, Oct. 1677; Judge (Guilford), 1676, 1677.
Conn. Col. II. 265, 274, 275, 286, 300, 304, 318.

CIVIL, MILITARY, AND ECCLESIASTICAL 33

LEETE, WILLIAM (d. 1683). Deputy (Guilford) to N. H. Leg., Oct. 1643, Apr. 1644; Secretary, N. H. Col., Oct. 1646; Assistant, N. H. Col., May 1653, May 1654, May 1655, May 1656, May 1657; Dep. Governor, N. H. Col., May 1658, May 1659, May 1660; Governor, N. H. Col., May 1661, May 1662, May 1663, May 1664; Commissioner to Mass. Col., June 1653, June 1654; Commissioner for United Colonies, May 1655, May 1656, May 1657, May 1658, May 1659, May 1660, May 1661, May 1662, May 1663, May 1664; Judge (Southold), May 1655; Assistant (provisional appointment, Conn. Col.), Oct. 1664; Assistant, Conn. Col., May 1665 to 1668 incl.; Commissioner for United Colonies, 1665, 1667, 1668, 1672, 1673; Moderator, 1668; Dep. Governor, 1669 to 1675 incl.; Governor, 1676, 1677; Commissioner to R. I., Oct. 1668, May 1670, May 1671; member of War Council, Nov. 1673, July 1675, May 1676. Granted 300 acres, Oct. 1667.
N. H. Col. I. 112, 129, 275. II. 1, 5, 91, 101, 140, 143, 168, 213, 231, 297, 359, 402, 450, 451, 488, 543. Conn. Col. I. 437. II. 13, 18, 30, 57, 68, 76, 82, 103, 104, 126, 134, 146, 156, 169, 170, 191, 192, 219, 220, 248, 261, 273, 284, 300.

LEETE, WILLIAM, JR. (d. 1687). Deputy (Guilford), May 1677.
Conn. Col. II. 300.

LEFFINGWELL, THOMAS (d. 1714). Granted 400 acres, Oct. 1667. Deputy (Norwich) to Conn. Leg., Oct. 1662, Oct. 1663, Oct. 1665, Oct. 1668, Oct. 1669, May 1670, Oct. 1670, May 1671, Oct. 1671, May 1672, Oct. 1672, May 1673, May 1674, Oct. 1674, May 1676, Oct. 1676, May 1677; called Sergeant, Oct. 1668; Ensign, Norwich Train Band, June 1672; in King Philip's War, Mar. 1676; Lieut., New London County Troop, May 1676, Aug. 1676.
Conn. Col. I. 384, 410. II. 24, 74, 94, 116, 126, 136, 147, 159, 170, 181, 184, 192, 221, 236, 274, 279, 286, 300, 418, 474.

LEWIS, WILLIAM, SR. (d. 1683). Granted 200 acres, May 1675, whereof he had 100 recorded to his grandson Philip Lewis.
Conn. Col. II. 254.

LEWIS, WILLIAM, JR. (d. 1690). Sergeant, Farmington Train Band, May 1649; Lieut. of same, Oct. 1651; Capt., Oct. 1674. Granted 200 acres, Oct. 1668.
Conn. Col. I. 187, 227. II. 101, 238.

LINDON, HENRY (d. 1660). Ensign, Artillery Co., May 1648; Ensign, New Haven Train Band, May 1652; Deputy (New Haven) to N. H. Leg., May 1653, May 1654, May 1659; Judge (New Haven), May 1651, May 1652, May 1653, May 1654, May 1655, May 1656, May 1657, May 1658, May 1659, May 1660.
N. H. Col. I. 382. II. 2, 92, 297. N. H. Town I. 72, 127, 180, 212, 240, 277, 313, 353, 402, 453.

List of Officials

LIVERMORE, JOHN (d. 1684). First called Corporal (New Haven Train Band), Apr. 1646 (resigned May 1647). (Removed to Watertown, Mass.)
N. H. Col. I. 230, 313.

LOCKWOOD, JONATHAN (d. 1688). Deputy (Greenwich), May 1671, Oct. 1671, May 1673, Oct. 1674, Oct. 1676; Commissioner on N. Y. Boundary, Oct. 1674; called Sergeant, 1673, and Lieut., 1674.
Conn. Col. II. 147, 160, 192, 236, 242, 287.

LOCKWOOD, ROBERT (d. 1658). Sergeant, Fairfield Train Band, May 1657.
Conn. Col. I. 299.

LOOMIS, JOHN (d. 1688). Deputy (Windsor), May 1666, Oct. 1666, May 1667, May 1675, May 1676, Oct. 1676, May 1677, Oct. 1677.
Conn. Col. II. 31, 46, 58, 248, 274, 286, 300.

LORD, RICHARD (d. 1662). Deputy (Hartford) to Conn. Leg., Feb. 1657, Aug. 1657, Oct. 1657, May 1658, Oct. 1658, May 1659, Oct. 1659, Oct. 1660, May 1661; Capt., Conn. Col. Troop, Mar. 1658; Patentee, Royal Charter, 1662.
Conn. Col. I. 288, 300, 306, 309, 315, 323, 334, 340, 353, 365. II. 4.

LORD, RICHARD, JR. (d. 1685-6). Deputy (Hartford), May 1669, Oct. 1669, May 1670, Oct. 1670, May 1671, Oct. 1671, May 1672, Oct. 1673, May 1674, Oct. 1674, May 1675, Oct. 1675, Oct. 1676; member of War Council, July 1675, May 1676.
Conn. Col. II. 105, 115, 126, 136, 147, 159, 169, 209, 221, 235, 248, 261, 264, 284, 286.

LUDLOW, ROGER (d. after 1664). Commissioner appointed by Mass. to govern Conn., Mar. 1636; Assistant, Conn. Col., Apr. 1636, Sept. 1636, Mar. 1637, May 1637, Nov. 1637, Feb. 1638, Mar. 1638, Apr. 1638, Apr. 1640, Apr. 1641, Apr. 1643, Apr. 1644, Apr. 1645, Apr. 1646, May 1647, May 1649, May 1650, May 1651, May 1652, May 1653; Dep. Governor, Conn. Col., Apr. 1639, Apr. 1642, May 1648; Commissioner to Saybrook, Pequot War, June 1637; Commissioner for United Colonies, May 1648, May 1651, May 1652, May 1653.
Hazard's State Papers I. 321. Conn. Col. I. 1, 3, 8, 9, 10, 11, 13, 17, 27, 46, 64, 71, 84, 103, 124, 137, 149, 163, 164, 185, 207, 218, 222, 231, 233, 240, 241.

MALBON, RICHARD. Judge (New Haven), Apr. 1642, Oct. 1642, Apr. 1643, Oct. 1643, Mar. 1644, Oct. 1644, Mar. 1645, Oct. 1645 (declined); Deputy (New Haven) to N. H. Leg., Mar. 1644, Oct. 1644, Mar. 1645, Oct. 1645 (declined); Assistant, N. H. Col., Oct. 1646. Capt., Artillery Co., Mar. 1645. (Returned to England.)
N. H. Col. I. 69, 78, 85, 119, 125, 129, 147, 148, 156, 158, 171, 173, 275.

MALTBY, WILLIAM (d. 1710). Cornet, New Haven County Troop, May 1673. (Residence, Branford.)
Conn. Col. II. 199.

Civil, Military, and Ecclesiastical 35

MANSFIELD, MOSES (d. 1703). Lieut., New Haven County Troop, Jan. 1676, May 1676, and Capt., May 1676, Aug. 1676; Lieut., New Haven Train Band, Oct. 1676; Deputy (New Haven), Oct. 1676, May 1677, Oct. 1677.
> Conn. Col. II. 279, 286, 292, 300, 318, 400, 443, 468.

MARSHALL, SAMUEL (d. 1675). Corporal, Conn. Col. Troop, Mar. 1658; Quartermaster, May 1673, granted 150 acres; Ensign, Hartford County Dragoons, Aug. 1675; Ensign, Hartford County Troop, Oct. 1675; Capt. in Army, King Philip's War, Nov. 1675. (Residence, Windsor.)
> Conn. Col. I. 309. II. 101, 193, 267, 356, 387.

MARSHALL, THOMAS. Deputy (Windsor) to Conn. Leg., Mar. 1638, Apr. 1638.
> Conn. Col. I. 13, 17.

MARTIN, ANTHONY (d. 1673). Corporal, to accompany Capt. Pynchon from Springfield to Fort Albany, July 1666. (Residence, Middletown.)
> Conn. Col. II. 43.

MARTIN, SAMUEL, SR. (d. 1683). Granted 150 acres, Oct. 1673. Peace messenger to N. Y., May 1674; Corporal in King Philip's War, July 1675; Lieut., Hartford County Troop, Jan. 1676. Granted 50 acres, Oct. 1677.
> Conn. Col. II. 214, 222, 327, 331, 400.

MARVIN, MATTHEW (d. 1680). Deputy (Norwalk) to Conn. Leg., May 1654.
> Conn. Col. I. 256.

MARVIN, REINOLD (d. 1676). Sergeant, Saybrook Train Band, Oct. 1661. Deputy for Lyme, Oct. 1670, Oct. 1672, May 1673, Oct. 1673, May 1674, Oct. 1674, Oct. 1675, May 1676. Called Lieut., Oct. 1675.
> Conn. Col. I. 375. II. 136, 184, 192, 204, 209, 221, 236, 265, 274.

MASON, DANIEL (d. 1736). Quartermaster, New London County Troop, Oct. 1673.
> Conn. Col. II. 214.

MASON, JOHN (d. 1672). Capt. in the Pequot War; first called Major, June 1654; War Committee for Saybrook, May 1653, Oct. 1654; Major, Conn. Col. Troop, Mar. 1658. Deputy (Windsor) to Conn. Leg., Nov. 1637, Mar. 1638, Apr. 1638, Sept. 1639, Feb. 1641, Apr. 1641, Sept. 1641; Assistant, Conn. Col., Apr. 1642, Apr. 1643, Apr. 1644, Apr. 1645, Apr. 1646, May 1647, May 1648, May 1649, May 1650, May 1651, May 1652, May 1653, May 1654, May 1655, May 1656, May 1657, May 1658, May 1659, 1669, 1670, 1671; Dep.

Governor, Conn. Col., May 1660, May 1661, May 1662, Oct. 1662, May 1663, May 1664, May 1665, May 1666, May 1667, May 1668; Patentee, Royal Charter, 1662; Commissioner for United Colonies, June 1654, May 1655, May 1656, May 1657, May 1660, May 1661; Commissioner to treat with N. H. Col., Mar. 1663, Aug. 1663; Commissioner for Mass. and R. I. Boundaries, Oct. 1664; Militia Committee, May 1667 to June 1672; granted 300 acres for one of his sons, May 1668.

Conn. Col. I. 9, 11, 13, 17, 34, 58, 64, 67, 71, 84, 103, 124, 137, 149, 163, 185, 207, 218, 231, 240, 243, 256, 259, 264, 274, 280, 281, 297, 299, 309, 314, 334, 347, 348, 364, 365, 378, 384, 396, 398, 407, 425, 435. II. 4, 13, 30, 57, 69, 82, 86, 104, 126, 146, 182.

MASON, JOHN, JR. (d. 1676). Ensign, Norwich Train Band, May 1669; Lieut. of same, June 1672; Capt. in command of Mohegans and Pequots, Sept. 1675; third in command of Army, Nov. 1675; Judge (Norwich), 1672, 1673, 1674, 1675; Deputy (Norwich), Oct. 1672, Oct. 1674, May 1675; Assistant, 1676; member of Council of War, May 1676.

Conn. Col. II. 107, 170, 181, 184, 192, 221, 236, 249, 250, 274, 284, 366, 386.

MASON, SAMUEL (d. 1705). Lieut., Stonington Train Band, May 1670; member of New London County Court Martial, Jan. 1677.

Conn. Col. II. 132, 484.

MAUDSLEY, JOHN (d. 1690). Ensign, Hartford County Troop, June 1676; Lieut. of same, Sept. 1677. (Residence, Windsor.)

Conn. Col. II. 458, 506.

MEAD, JOSEPH (d. 1690). Deputy (Greenwich), Oct. 1669, May 1670, May 1671.

Conn. Col. II. 116, 127, 147.

MEAD, WILLIAM (d. after 1669). Deputy (New London) to Conn. Leg., Oct. 1653.

Conn. Col. I. 248.

MEASURE, WILLIAM (d. 1688). Deputy (Lyme), May 1676, May 1677.

Conn. Col. II. 274, 300.

MEIGS, JOHN (d. 1672). Clerk, New Haven Train Band, May 1648. Dep. Judge (Guilford), May 1663.

N. H. Col. I. 382. Conn. Col. I. 405.

MERRIMAN, NATHANIEL (d. 1694). Served in the Pequot War; Sergeant, Artillery Co. (prior to 1664); Ensign, New Haven Train Band, May 1664; confirmed Sergeant of same, July 1665. Lieut., Wallingford Train Band, May 1672; Capt., New Haven County Dragoons, Nov. 1675. Deputy (Wallingford), May 1674.

N. H. Town II. 89. Conn. Col. II. 23, 172, 221, 379.

MILES, JOHN (d. 1704). Ensign, New Haven Train Band, Oct. 1673; Ensign, King Philip's War, Sept. 1675; seventh in command of Army, Nov. 1675.
Conn. Col. II. 214, 364, 386.

MILES, RICHARD (d. 1667). Judge (New Haven), May 1648, May 1649, May 1650, May 1651, May 1652; Deputy (New Haven) to N. H. Leg., May 1651; Clerk, Artillery Co., May 1648.
N. H. Col. I. 381, 382, 456. N. H. Town I. 21, 72, 127.

MINER, EPHRAIM (d. 1724). Deputy (Stonington), Oct. 1676, Oct. 1677.
Conn. Col. II. 286, 318.

MINER, JOHN (d. 1719). Deputy (Stratford), Oct. 1676, and then called Capt. (Removed to Woodbury.)
Conn. Col. II. 286.

MINER, THOMAS (d. 1690). Sergeant, New London Train Band, May 1649; Chief Military Officer, Mystic Train Band, July 1665; Deputy (New London) to Conn. Leg., Sept. 1650, May 1651, Sept. 1651; Deputy (Stonington), May 1665, Oct. 1665, Oct. 1667, Oct. 1670, Oct. 1672, May 1677; Judge (New London), May 1649; Judge (Stonington), Oct. 1664, May 1665, 1669 to 1677 incl. Lieut. in King Philip's War, Feb. and Apr. 1676; Capt., Aug. 1676; Committee on Indians, Oct. 1676; member of New London County Court Martial, Jan. 1677. Granted 100 acres, May 1666, and 50 acres, Oct. 1667.
Conn. Col. I. 187, 211, 218, 224, 435. II. 14, 17, 22, 24, 36, 70, 74, 106, 131, 136, 152, 170, 184, 193, 221, 250, 275, 287, 300, 304, 407, 429, 468, 484.

MITCHELL, MATTHEW (d. 1645). Deputy (Wethersfield) to Conn. Leg., May 1637; Assistant, Conn. Col., Nov. 1637, Feb. 1638, Mar. 1638, Apr. 1638; Dep. Judge (Stamford), Apr. 1643.
Conn. Col. I. 9, 11, 13, 17. N. H. Col. I. 85.

MOODY, JOHN (d. 1655). Lieut., Hartford Train Band, Apr. 1640.
Conn. Col. I. 48.

MOORE, ISAAC (d. after 1694). Sergeant, Farmington Train Band, May 1649; Deputy (Farmington) to Conn. Leg., Oct. 1657.
Conn. Col. I. 187, 306, 440.

MOORE, JOHN (d. 1677). Deputy (Windsor) to Conn. Leg., Sept. 1653, May 1661, Oct. 1661, May 1662, Oct. 1664, May 1665, Oct. 1665, Oct. 1666, May 1667, Oct. 1667, May 1668, Oct. 1668, May 1669, Oct. 1669, May 1670, Oct. 1670, May 1671, Oct. 1671, May 1672, Oct. 1672, May 1673, Oct. 1673, May 1674, Oct. 1674, May 1675, Oct. 1675, May 1676, Oct. 1676, May 1677.
Conn. Col. I. 246, 365, 372, 378, 431. II. 13, 23, 46, 58, 69, 82, 94, 105, 116, 126, 136, 147, 159, 169, 183, 192, 209, 221, 235, 248, 264, 274, 286, 300.

LIST OF OFFICIALS

MOORE, THOMAS (d. 1691). Deputy (Southold) to N. H. Leg., May 1658; Judge (Southold), May 1658.
N. H. Col. II. 232, 236.

MOREHOUSE, JOHN (d. 1701). Ensign, Fairfield County Troop, May 1676. (Removed to Southampton, L. I.)
Conn. Col. II. 279.

MOREHOUSE, THOMAS (d. 1658). Deputy (Fairfield) to Conn. Leg., Sept. 1653.
Conn. Col. I. 246.

MORGAN, JAMES (d. 1685). Deputy (New London) to Conn. Leg., May 1657, Oct. 1658, Oct. 1661, May 1663, Oct. 1663, May 1665, Oct. 1665, Oct. 1666, May 1670; Committee on Stonington Indians, Oct. 1666.
Conn. Col. I. 297, 323, 372, 399, 410. II. 13, 24, 47, 56, 127.

MOSS, JOHN (d. 1707). Corporal, New Haven Train Band, Aug. 1642 (resigned May 1652). Deputy (New Haven) to N. H. Leg., May 1664; to Conn. Leg., May 1667, Oct. 1667, May 1668, Oct. 1668, May 1669, Oct. 1669, May 1670, Oct. 1670; Deputy (Wallingford), May 1671, May 1672, Oct. 1672, May 1673, Oct. 1673, Oct. 1675, May 1676, Oct. 1676, May 1677, Oct. 1677; Judge (Wallingford), 1672, 1673, 1674, 1675, 1676, 1677.
N. H. Col. I. 76. II. 544. N. H. Town I. 127. Conn. Col. II. 58, 69, 83, 94, 105, 115, 126, 136, 147, 169, 170, 184, 192, 193, 209, 221, 250, 265, 274, 276, 286, 300, 304, 318.

MOXON, GEORGE (REV.) (d. 1687). Deputy (Springfield) to Conn. Leg., Apr. 1638. (Returned to England.)
Conn. Col. I. 17.

MULFORD, JOHN (d. 1686). Assistant, Conn. Col., May 1658; Judge (East Hampton), May 1664, May 1674.
Conn. Col. I. 314, 428. II. 229.

MUNN, BENJAMIN (d. 1675). Served in Pequot War. (Removed to Springfield.) Lot in Soldiers' Field, Hartford.

MUNSON, SAMUEL (d. 1692). Ensign, Wallingford Train Band, Oct. 1675.
Conn. Col. II. 271.

MUNSON, THOMAS (d. 1686). Served in the Pequot War; Sergeant, New Haven Train Band, Aug. 1642; Sergeant, Artillery Co., Mar. 1645; Sergeant, N. H. Col. Troop, June 1654; Ensign, New Haven Train Band, Mar. 1661 (declined, but accepted as acting Ensign); Lieut. of same, May 1664, confirmed July 1665. Deputy (New Haven) to N. H. Leg., May 1663, May 1664; Judge (New Haven), June 1662, May 1663, May 1664. Deputy (New Haven), May 1666, May 1669, Oct. 1669, May 1670, Oct. 1670, May 1671, Oct. 1671, May

Civil, Military, and Ecclesiastical 39

1672, Oct. 1672, May 1673, Oct. 1673, May 1674, Oct. 1674, May 1675, May 1676, Oct. 1676, May 1677, Oct. 1677; War Committee, Aug. 1673; member of War Council, Nov. 1673; Lieut., New Haven County Troop, Aug. 1673; Lieut., New Haven County Dragoons, Sept. 1675; Capt., New Haven County Troop, Feb. 1676. Granted 100 acres, May 1673.

N. H. Col. I. 76, 158. II. 108, 488, 544. N. H. Town I. 474, 523. II. 45, 88, 89. Conn. Col. II. 23, 31, 105, 115, 126, 136, 147, 160, 169, 183, 192, 196, 204, 206, 209, 219, 221, 235, 249, 274, 279, 286, 300, 318, 367, 411.

MYGATT, JOSEPH (d. 1680). Deputy (Hartford) to Conn. Leg., Oct. 1656, Feb. 1657, Aug. 1657, Oct. 1657, May 1658, Oct. 1658, May 1659, Oct. 1659, May 1660, Oct. 1660, May 1661, Oct. 1661, May 1662.

Conn. Col. I. 282, 288, 300, 306, 315, 323, 334, 340, 347, 353, 365, 372, 378.

NASH, JOHN (d. 1687). Corporal, New Haven Train Band, Aug. 1642; Sergeant of same, July 1644; Sergeant, Artillery Co., Mar. 1645, May 1648; Lieut., New Haven Train Band, June 1652; Lieut. (chief military officer), Mar. 1654; Lieut., N. H. Col. Troop, June 1654; nominated Capt., Mar. 1661 (declined); Capt., New Haven Train Band, May 1664, confirmed July 1665. Deputy (New Haven) to N. H. Leg., May 1659, May 1660, May 1661, May 1663, Oct. 1663, Jan. 1664; Assistant, N. H. Col., May 1664 (declined); Judge (New Haven), May 1653 to 1670 incl. Deputy (New Haven) to Conn. Leg., May 1665; Assistant, 1672 to 1677 incl. Chief Military Officer, New Haven County, June 1672; Capt., New Haven County Troop, Nov. 1673; member of War Council, Nov. 1673, July 1675, May 1676. Granted 300 acres, Oct. 1674.

N. H. Col. I. 76, 141, 158, 382. II. 52, 108, 297, 403, 477, 500, 513, 543. N. H. Town I. 131, 180, 212, 240, 277, 313, 353, 402, 453, 474, 484, 485, 523. II. 40, 45, 89, 142. Conn. Col. II. 13, 18, 22, 32, 63, 84, 106, 131, 169, 183, 218, 219, 221, 241, 248, 261, 274, 284, 300.

NASH, JOSEPH (d. 1678). Corporal, New Haven Train Band, May 1647. Sealer of Weights, Oct. 1670; called Sergeant.

N. H. Col. I. 313. Conn. Col. II. 141.

NEWBERRY, BENJAMIN (d. 1689). Deputy (Windsor) to Conn. Leg., May 1656, Oct. 1656, May 1662, May 1663, Oct. 1663, Oct. 1664, May 1665, Oct. 1665, May 1666, Oct. 1667, May 1668, Oct. 1668, May 1669, Oct. 1669, May 1670, Oct. 1670, May 1671, Oct. 1671, May 1672, Oct. 1672, May 1673, Oct. 1673, May 1674, Oct. 1674, Oct. 1675, Oct. 1677; Judge (Windsor), 1669, (Windsor and Simsbury), 1670 to 1677 incl.; Commissioner for Mass. and R. I. Boundaries, Oct. 1664; first called Captain, May 1662; Second Military Officer, Hartford County, June 1672; Capt., Hartford County Troop, Aug. 1673, Aug. 1675; second in command of Army, King

Philip's War, Nov. 1675 (not able to go); Capt., Hartford County Troop, June 1676; Committee on Stonington and Indian bounds, May 1666; Militia Committee, July 1666; Commissioner to R. I., May 1670; War Committee, Aug. 1673; member of War Council, Nov. 1673, July 1675, May 1676. Granted 250 acres, Oct. 1667.
Conn. Col. I. 281, 282, 378, 399, 409, 431, 435. II. 13, 23, 31, 33, 44, 69, 77, 82, 94, 105, 106, 116, 126, 130, 134, 136, 147, 152, 159, 169, 170, 183, 192, 204, 206, 209, 219, 221, 235, 250, 261, 284, 304, 318, 347, 386, 387, 458.

NEWMAN, FRANCIS (d. 1660). Ensign, New Haven Train Band, Aug. 1642; Lieut. (Ensign), Artillery Co., Mar. 1645; Lieut., New Haven Train Band, May 1652 (resigned June 1652). Judge (New Haven), Mar. 1645, Oct. 1645, Oct. 1646, Oct. 1647, May 1648, May 1649, May 1650, May 1651, May 1652; Deputy (New Haven) to N. H. Leg., Oct. 1647, May 1649, Sept. 1649, May 1650, May 1651, May 1652; Assistant, N. H. Col., May 1653, May 1654, May 1655, May 1656, May 1657; Secretary, N. H. Col., May 1653, May 1654, May 1655, May 1656, May 1657; Governor, N. H. Col., May 1658, May 1659, May 1660; Commissioner for United Colonies, July 1654, May 1658, May 1659, May 1660.
N. H. Col. I. 76, 156, 158, 171, 274, 354, 381, 456, 481. II. 1, 91, 92, 111, 140, 168, 213, 231, 297, 359. N. H. Town I. 21, 72, 127, 131.

NEWMAN, ROBERT. Judge (New Haven), Oct. 1639, Oct. 1640, May 1641, Oct. 1641. (Returned to England.)
N. H. Col. I. 21, 44, 51, 58.

NEWTON, ROGER (REV.) (d. 1683). Minister at Farmington, 1652–1657; at Milford, 1660–1683.

NEWTON, SAMUEL (d. 1708). Ensign, New Haven County Troop, Aug. 1673. (Residence, Milford.)
Conn. Col. II. 206.

NEWTON, THOMAS (d. in or before 1683). Deputy (Fairfield) to Conn. Leg., Apr. 1645.
Conn. Col. I. 124.

NICHOLS, FRANCIS (d. 1650). Sergeant, Stratford Train Band, Oct. 1639.
Conn. Col. I. 36.

NICHOLS, ISAAC (d. 1695). Deputy (Stratford) to Conn. Leg., May 1662, Oct. 1664.
Conn. Col. I. 379, 431.

NOBLE, WILLIAM. Judge (Flushing), May 1664.
Conn. Col. I. 428.

NOTT, JOHN (d. 1682). Sergeant, Wethersfield Train Band, May 1657. Deputy (Wethersfield) to Conn. Leg., May 1662, Oct. 1662,

CIVIL, MILITARY, AND ECCLESIASTICAL 41

May 1663, Oct. 1663, May 1664, Oct. 1664, Oct. 1665, May 1666, Oct. 1666, May 1667, Oct. 1667, May 1668, Oct. 1668, May 1669, Oct. 1669, May 1670, Oct. 1670, May 1671, Oct. 1671, Oct. 1674. Granted 50 acres, May 1670 (for Pequot War service).
Conn. Col. I. 299, 378, 384, 399, 409, 425, 431. II. 24, 31, 47, 58, 69, 82, 94, 105, 115, 127, 133, 136, 147, 159, 235.

NOYES, JAMES (REV.) (d. 1719). Harvard College, 1659. Minister at Stonington, 1666–1719. Chaplain, King Philip's War, Dec. 1675 (not able to go).
Conn. Col. II. 388.

NOYES, NICHOLAS (REV.) (d. 1701). Chaplain, King Philip's War, Dec. 1675. (Residence, Newbury, Mass.)
Conn. Col. II. 388.

OGDEN, JOHN (d. 1682). Assistant, Conn. Col., May 1656, May 1657, May 1658, May 1659, May 1660, Oct. 1662; Patentee, Royal Charter, 1662; Deputy (Rye), Oct. 1674.
Conn. Col. I. 280, 297, 314, 334, 347, 384. II. 4, 236.

OLCOTT, THOMAS (d. 1654). Served in Pequot War. Lot in Soldiers' Field, Hartford.

OLMSTEAD, JOHN (d. 1686). Surgeon, King Philip's War, May 1676. (Residence, Norwich.)
Conn. Col. II. 286, 483.

OLMSTEAD, JOHN (d. 1704). Ensign, Norwalk Train Band, May 1674.
Conn. Col. II. 223.

OLMSTEAD, NEHEMIAH (d. 1657). Sergeant, Fairfield Train Band, May 1657.
Conn. Col. I. 299.

OLMSTEAD, NICHOLAS (d. 1684). Served in the Pequot War; Corporal, Conn. Col. Troop, Mar. 1658. Deputy (Hartford), Oct. 1672, May 1673; called Ensign, Oct. 1672; Lieut., Hartford County Troop, Aug. 1673; Lieut., Hartford Train Band, Oct. 1673 (declined); Lieut., King Philip's War, July 1675; Capt., Hartford County Dragoons, Aug. 1675.
Conn. Col. I. 309. II. 183, 192, 206, 210, 332, 355.

OLMSTEAD, RICHARD (d. 1687). Sergeant, Norwalk Train Band, May 1653; Sergeant, Conn. Col. Troop, May 1653; Lieut., Norwalk Train Band, May 1659. Deputy (Norwalk) to Conn. Leg., May 1653, Sept. 1654, May 1658, Oct. 1660, May 1661, May 1662, May 1663, Oct. 1663, May 1664, Oct. 1664, Oct. 1665, May 1666, Oct. 1666, May 1667, May 1668, Oct. 1668, May 1669, May 1671; Judge (Norwalk), 1668 to 1677 incl.; Muster Master, Fairfield County,

Nov. 1673. Granted 60 acres, May 1669 (for Pequot War service).
Conn. Col. I. 240, 242, 243, 264, 315, 336, 354, 365, 379, 399, 410, 425, 432. II. 24, 31, 47, 59, 83, 84, 94, 105, 106, 113, 131, 147, 152, 170, 193, 218, 221, 250, 276, 304.

ORTON, JOSEPH, see HORTON.

OSBORN, JEREMIAH (d. 1676). Deputy (New Haven), Oct. 1672, May 1673, Oct. 1673, May 1674, May 1675, Oct. 1675; called Sergeant, Oct. 1675.
Conn. Col. II. 183, 192, 209, 221, 249, 265.

OSBORN, RICHARD (d. 1684). Granted 80 acres for Pequot War service, May 1671. (Residence, Fairfield.)
Conn. Col. II. 151.

PALMER, NEHEMIAH (d. 1717). Deputy (Stonington), May 1668, Oct. 1668, May 1669, May 1674, Oct. 1674, May 1676.
Conn. Col. II. 83, 94, 105, 221, 236, 274.

PALMER, NICHOLAS (d. 1689). Served in Pequot War.
Mason's *Narrative*.

PALMES, EDWARD (d. 1715). Judge (New London), 1664, 1667, 1671, 1672, 1673, 1674, 1675, 1676, 1677; Magistrate, New London County and the Narragansett Country, May 1674; Deputy (New London), May 1671, Oct. 1671, May 1672, May 1673, Oct. 1673, May 1674, Oct. 1674, Oct. 1677; Militia Committee, June 1672; Capt., New London County Troop, Oct. 1672; called Capt., Oct. 1673, and Major, May 1674; member of New London County Court Martial, Jan. 1677. Granted 200 acres, Oct. 1673.
Conn. Col. I. 426. II. 63, 147, 152, 169, 170, 182, 186, 192, 209, 214, 221, 231, 235, 250, 275, 304, 318, 484.

PARKE, ROBERT (d. 1665). Served in Pequot War. Deputy (Wethersfield) to Conn. Leg., Aug. 1642; Deputy (New London), May 1652.
Conn. Col. I. 73, 231. Shepard.

PARKER, WILLIAM (d. 1686). Deputy (Saybrook) to Conn. Leg., Sept. 1652, May 1672, May 1673, Oct. 1673, Oct. 1674, May 1676; called Sergeant, May 1672. Granted 100 acres, May 1673 (for Pequot War service).
Conn. Col. I. 235. II. 169, 192, 196, 209, 236, 274.

PARSONS, THOMAS (d. 1661). Served in Pequot War. (Residence, Windsor.)
Conn. Col. IV. 277.

PATTERSON, EDWARD (d. 1670). Granted 60 acres, May 1670 (for Pequot War service). (Residence, East Haven.)
Conn. Col. II. 130.

CIVIL, MILITARY, AND ECCLESIASTICAL 43

PEAKIN, JOHN. Deputy (Southold) to N. H. Leg., May 1654; Judge (Southold), May 1654.
N. H. Col. II. 92, 95.

PECK, JEREMIAH (REV.) (d. 1699). Preached at Guilford, 1656–1660; minister at Elizabethtown, N. J., 1670–1678; at Greenwich, 1678–1689; at Waterbury, 1691–1699.

PECK, JOSEPH (d. 1718). Deputy (Lyme), Oct. 1676.
Conn. Col. II. 286.

PELL, THOMAS (DR.) (d. 1669). Served in the Pequot War. Judge (Fairfield), May 1661; Deputy (Fairfield) to Conn. Leg., May 1664, May 1665.
Conn. Col. I. 366, 425. II. 13.

PERRY, RICHARD. Clerk, New Haven Train Band, July 1644. (Returned to England.)
N. H. Col. I. 141.

PHELPS, WILLIAM (d. 1672). Commissioner appointed by Mass. to govern Conn., Mar. 1636; Assistant, Conn. Col., Apr. 1636, Sept. 1636, Mar. 1637, May 1637, Nov. 1637, Mar. 1638, Apr. 1638, Apr. 1639, Apr. 1640, Apr. 1641, Apr. 1642; Deputy (Windsor) to Conn. Leg., Apr. 1645, Sept. 1645, Apr. 1646, Oct. 1646, May 1647, Sept. 1647, May 1648, Sept. 1648, May 1649, Sept. 1649, Sept. 1650, May 1651, Sept. 1651, May 1652, Sept. 1652, May 1653, Oct. 1653, May 1654, Sept. 1654, May 1655, Feb. 1657, May 1657, Oct. 1657; Assistant, Conn. Col., May 1658, May 1659, May 1660, May 1661, May 1662; War Committee for Windsor, May 1653, Oct. 1654.
Hazard's State Papers I. 321. Conn. Col. I. 1, 3, 8, 9, 11, 13, 17, 27, 46, 64, 71, 124, 130, 138, 145, 149, 157, 163, 166, 185, 195, 211, 218, 224, 231, 235, 240, 243, 247, 256, 263, 264, 274, 288, 297, 306, 314, 334, 347, 365, 378.

PHILLIPS, WILLIAM (d 1655). Served in Pequot War. Lot in Soldiers' Field, Hartford.

PICKETT, JOHN (d. 1684). Deputy (Stratford), May 1673, May 1675.
Conn. Col. II. 192, 249.

PIERCE, JOHN (d. 1661). Served in Pequot War. Lot in Soldiers' Field, Hartford.

PIERCE, THOMAS. Judge (Setauket), May 1661.
Conn. Col. I. 366.

PIERSON, ABRAHAM (REV.) (d. 1678). Minister at Southampton, L. I.; at Branford, 1647–1666; at Newark, N. J., 1666–1678. Chaplain, N. H. Col. Troop, June 1654.
N. H. Col. II. 108.

PIPER, RICHARD (d. 1678). Deputy (Haddam), May 1674.
Conn. Col. II. 221.

PITKIN, WILLIAM (d. 1694). Deputy (Hartford), Oct. 1675, May 1676, Oct. 1676, (Hartford and Greenwich), May 1677, Oct. 1677; Treasurer, 1676, 1677; Agent to N. Y., Apr. 1676; Committee on Indians, Oct. 1676.
Conn. Col. II. 264, 274, 280, 286, 287, 300, 311, 318, 426.

PLUMB, JOHN (d. 1648). Served in the Pequot War. Assistant, Conn. Col., Feb. 1638, Mar. 1638, Apr. 1638; Deputy (Wethersfield) to Conn. Leg., Nov. 1641, Apr. 1642, Mar. 1643.
Conn. Col. I. 11, 13, 17, 69, 71, 82.

PLUMB, JOHN (d. 1728). Granted 80 acres, Oct. 1674.
Conn. Col. II. 241.

PORTER, DANIEL (DR.) (d. 1688 to 1690). Granted 100 acres, Oct. 1669; salary augmented from £6 to £12 a year for service of the country in setting bones, May 1671. (Residence, Farmington.)
Conn. Col. II. 123, 153.

PORTER, JOHN (d. 1648). Deputy (Windsor) to Conn. Leg., Aug. 1639, Oct. 1646, May 1647.
Conn. Col. I. 29, 145, 149.

PORTER, JOHN (d. 1688). Granted 120 acres, May 1674. (Residence, Windsor.)
Conn. Col. II. 230.

POST, ABRAHAM (d. 1706). Ensign, Saybrook Train Band, May 1667.
Conn. Col. II. 60.

PRATT, JOHN (d. 1655). Deputy (Hartford) to Conn. Leg., Aug. 1639, Sept. 1639, Jan. 1640, Feb. 1641, Apr. 1641, Sept. 1641, Nov. 1641, May 1655.
Conn. Col. I. 29, 34, 41, 58, 64, 67, 69, 274.

PRATT, WILLIAM (d. c. 1678). Lieut., Saybrook Train Band, Oct. 1661. Judge (Saybrook), 1666, 1667, (Saybrook and Lyme), 1668, 1669, 1670, 1671, 1672, 1673, 1674, 1675, 1676, 1677; Deputy (Saybrook), Oct. 1666, Oct. 1667, Oct. 1668, May 1669, Oct. 1669, Oct. 1670, May 1671, Oct. 1671, May 1672, May 1673, Oct. 1673, May 1674, Oct. 1674, May 1675, Oct. 1675, May 1676, Oct. 1676, May 1677, Oct. 1677; granted 100 acres, Oct. 1670 (for Pequot War service).
Conn. Col. I. 375. II. 32, 47, 63, 70, 84, 94, 105, 106, 116, 131, 136, 144, 147, 152, 159, 169, 170, 192, 209, 221, 236, 249, 250, 265, 274, 275, 286, 300, 304, 318.

PRENTICE, JOHN (d. 1691). Deputy (New London), Oct. 1668, Oct. 1670.
Conn. Col. II. 94, 136.

CIVIL, MILITARY, AND ECCLESIASTICAL 45

PRESTON, JEHIEL (d. 1684). Deputy (Stratford), May 1676.
Conn. Col. II. 274.

PRUDDEN, PETER (REV.) (d. 1656). Minister at Milford, 1639–1656.

PURKAS, JOHN (d. 1645). Served in Pequot War. Lot in Soldiers' Field, Hartford.

PURRIER, WILLIAM (d. 1676). Deputy (Southold) to N. H. Leg., June 1653, May 1656, May 1661; Judge (Southold), May 1656.
N. H. Col. II. 4, 169, 172, 403.

PYNCHON, JOHN (MAJ.) (d. 1703). Commissioner to N. Y., Apr. 1677. (Residence, Springfield.)
Conn. Col. II. 490.

PYNCHON, WILLIAM (d. 1662). Commissioner appointed by Mass. to govern Conn., Mar. 1636; Assistant, Conn. Col., Nov. 1636, Mar. 1638, Apr. 1638; his shallop commandeered, Pequot War, May 1637. (Residence, Springfield, Mass.; returned to England.)
Hazard's State Papers I. 321. Conn. Col. I. 5, 10, 13, 17.

RATLIFF, WILLIAM (d. 1676). Deputy (Greenwich), May 1670.
Conn. Col. II. 127.

RAYMOND, JOSHUA (d. 1676). Cornet, New London County Troop, Oct. 1672.
Conn. Col. II. 186.

RAYNER, THURSTAN (d. 1667). Deputy (Wethersfield) to Conn. Leg., Mar. 1638, Apr. 1638, Apr. 1639, Jan. 1640, Apr. 1640; Judge (Stamford), Oct. 1641, Apr. 1643, Oct. 1643; Assistant, Conn. Col., May 1661, May 1663; Judge (Southampton), May 1664.
Conn. Col. I. 13, 17, 27, 41, 46, 365, 399, 428. N. H. Col. I. 58, 85, 112.

REYNOLDS, JONATHAN (d. 1673). Deputy (Greenwich), Oct. 1667.
Conn. Col. II. 70.

RICHARDS, JAMES (d. 1680). Assistant, Conn. Col., Oct. 1664, May 1665, 1669 to 1677 incl.; Lieut., Conn. Col. Troop, May 1664; Commissioner for United Colonies, 1672, 1674, 1675, 1676, 1677; Commissioner to R. I., May 1670, Oct. 1670, May 1671, May 1672; Committee for Indian Controversy, May 1671; Commissioner to Dutch Commanders, Aug. 1673; member of War Council, Nov. 1673, July 1675, May 1676; Agent to England, July 1675, Sept. 1677; Commissioner to N. Y., Apr. 1677. Granted 300 acres, May 1671.
Conn. Col. I. 429, 435. II. 13, 105, 126, 134, 146, 151, 156, 157, 169, 170, 173, 191, 206, 219, 221, 248, 261, 263, 274, 275, 284, 300, 301, 492, 504.

RICHARDS, NATHANIEL (d. 1682). Deputy (Norwalk) to Conn. Leg., Oct. 1658.
Conn. Col. I. 323.

RICHARDSON, AMOS (d. 1683). Deputy (Stonington), Oct. 1676, May 1677, Oct. 1677.
Conn. Col. II. 286, 300, 318.

RICHBELL, JOHN. Judge (Oyster Bay), May 1664.
Conn. Col. I. 428.

ROBBINS, JOHN (d. 1660). Deputy (Wethersfield) to Conn. Leg., Apr. 1643, Sept. 1643, Oct. 1656, Feb. 1657, May 1657, Oct. 1659.
Conn. Col. I. 84, 93, 282, 288, 297, 340.

ROGERS, JAMES (d. 1687). Deputy (New London) to Conn. Leg., May 1661, May 1662, Oct. 1662, May 1663, Oct. 1663, Oct. 1664, May 1666, Oct. 1668. Dep. Judge (New London), Apr. 1660, May 1660. Granted 200 acres in lieu of former grant of 150 acres, Oct. 1668; granted 50 acres, Oct. 1671 (for Pequot War service).
Conn. Col. I. 347, 352, 365, 379, 384, 399, 410, 432. II. 31, 94, 100, 161.

ROOT, THOMAS (d. 1694). Served in Pequot War. (Removed to Northampton.) Lot in Soldiers' Field, Hartford.

ROSE, ROBERT (d. 1665). Deputy (Wethersfield) to Conn. Leg., Sept. 1641, Aug. 1642, Mar. 1643, Apr. 1643.
Conn. Col. I. 67, 73, 82, 84. [No proof of service in Pequot War found.]

ROSE, ROBERT, JR. (d. 1683). Granted 50 acres, May 1668 (for service in Pequot War). (Residence, Stratford.)
Conn. Col. II. 85.

ROSEWELL, WILLIAM (d. 1694). Commissioner to Dutch Commanders, Aug. 1673; Capt., New Haven County Troop, May 1675, Oct. 1675.
Conn. Col. II. 206, 256, 268.

ROSSITER, BRAY (DR.) (d. 1672). Ensign, Windsor Train Band, Apr. 1640; Deputy (Windsor) to Conn. Leg., Apr. 1643, Sept. 1645.
Conn. Col. I. 48, 84, 130.

ROWLANDSON, JOSEPH (REV.) (d. 1678). Harvard College, 1652. Minister at Lancaster, Mass., 1656-1676; at Wethersfield, 1677-1678.

ROYCE, ROBERT (d. 1676). Deputy (New London) to Conn. Leg., May 1661.
Conn. Col. I. 365.

RUMBALL, THOMAS (d. *c.* 1649). Served in Pequot War. (Residence, Stratford.)
Lyon Gardiner's *Relation of the Pequot Wars*.

RUSSELL, JAMES (d. 1674). Clerk, New Haven Train Band, May 1658.
N. H. Town I. 354.

CIVIL, MILITARY, AND ECCLESIASTICAL 47

RUSSELL, JOHN (REV.) (d. 1692). Harvard College, 1645. Minister at Wethersfield, 1650–1659; at Hadley, Mass., 1660–1692.

RUSSELL, WILLIAM (d. 1665). Corporal, New Haven Train Band, May 1652; Sergeant of same, Mar. 1661.
N. H. Town I. 127, 474.

ST. JOHN, MARK (d. 1693). Deputy (Norwalk), Oct. 1672, Oct. 1676.
Conn. Col. II. 184, 286.

SANFORD, ROBERT (d. 1676). Granted 80 acres, Oct. 1672 (for service in Pequot War). (Residence, Hartford.)
Conn. Col. II. 189.

SANFORD, ZACHARIAH (d. 1668). Deputy (Saybrook), May 1667, May 1668.
Conn. Col. II. 58, 83.

SANFORD, ZACHARIAH (d. 1714). Sergeant, Hartford County Troop, Jan. 1676.
Conn. Col. II. 400.

SAUNDERS, GEORGE (d. 1690?). Ensign, Killingworth Train Band, Oct. 1667.
Conn. Col. II. 77.

SAUNDERS, TOBIAS (d. 1695). Judge (Stonington), Oct. 1670.
Conn. Col. II. 138.

SCRANTON, JOHN (d. 1671). Deputy (Guilford) to N. H. Leg., Jan. 1664; to Conn. Leg., Oct. 1669, May 1670.
N. H. Col. II. 513. Conn. Col. II. 116, 126.

SEELEY, NATHANIEL (d. 1675). Called Sergeant, May 1674; Lieut., second in command of Army, King Philip's War, Nov. 1675; Capt., Fairfield County Dragoons, Nov. 1675; sixth in command of Army, Nov. 1675 (called Robert by error).
Conn. Col. II. 223, 382, 386.

SEELEY, ROBERT (d. 1668). Lieut. (second in command under Mason), Pequot War, May 1637; Marshal (New Haven town), Oct. 1639 to Nov. 1642; Lieut., New Haven Train Band, Aug. 1642; Lieut., Artillery Co., Mar. 1645; Capt., Artillery Co., May 1648; Capt., N. H. Col. Troop, June 1654; in command of N. H. Col. Troops against Ninigret, Oct. 1654; Lieut. (chief military officer), Huntington Train Band, May 1663 (and referred to as Capt.); Judge (Huntington), May 1663, May 1664; Deputy (Huntington) to Conn. Leg., May 1664.
Conn. Col. I. 9, 401, 406, 425, 428. N. H. Col. I. 21, 44, 58, 76, 79, 80, 158, 382. II. 108, 118, 120.

SELLECK, JONATHAN (d. 1713). Deputy (Stamford), May 1670, May 1671, May 1672, May 1673, May 1675, May 1676; Peace messenger to N. Y., May 1674; Commissioner, N. Y. Boundary, Oct. 1674; called Lieut., May 1670; Capt., Stamford Train Band, July 1675; Capt., Fairfield County Troop, Jan. 1676; Capt., Fairfield County Troop, May 1676.
Conn. Col. II. 126, 147, 170, 192, 222, 242, 249, 261, 279, 400.

SEWARD, WILLIAM (d. 1689). Sergeant, Guilford Train Band, July 1665; Deputy (Guilford), Oct. 1673, Oct. 1674; called Lieut., Oct. 1673. Granted 100 acres, May 1673.
Conn. Col. II. 22, 200, 209, 236.

SHAW, THOMAS. 100 acres granted to his wife, May 1675. (Residence, Stonington.)
Conn. Col. II. 257.

SHEAF, JACOB (d. 1659). Deputy (Guilford) to N. H. Leg., Apr. 1644. (Removed to Boston.)
N. H. Col. I. 129.

SHERMAN, DANIEL (d. 1716). Ensign, New Haven County Troop, May 1676.
Conn. Col. II. 443.

SHERMAN, JOHN (REV.) (d. 1685). Deputy (Wethersfield) to Conn. Leg., May 1637; Deputy (Milford) to N. H. Leg., Oct. 1643. Probably preached at Wethersfield, 1636-1639. (Removed to Watertown, Mass.)
Conn. Col. I. 9. N. H. Col. I. 112.

SHERMAN, SAMUEL (d. 1700). Served in the Pequot War. Deputy (Stratford) to Conn. Leg., Oct. 1660; Assistant, Conn. Col., Oct. 1662 to 1667 incl.; Judge (Stratford), 1671 to 1675 incl., (Stratford and Woodbury), 1676, 1677.
Conn. Col. I. 354, 384, 425. II. 13, 30, 57, 152, 170, 193, 221, 250, 276, 304.

SHERWOOD, MATTHEW (d. 1715). Ensign, Fairfield County Troop, Aug. 1673.
Conn. Col. II. 206.

SHERWOOD, THOMAS (d. 1657). Deputy (Stratford) to Conn. Leg., Sept. 1645, Sept. 1649, May 1650, Oct. 1653, Oct. 1654; War Committee for Stratford, Oct. 1654.
Conn. Col. I. 130, 195, 207, 248, 261, 264 (twice called Sherratt).

SLAWSON, GEORGE (d. 1695). Judge (Stamford), May 1657; Dep. Judge (Stamford), May 1659; Deputy (Stamford) to N. H. Leg., Oct. 1663.
N. H. Col. II. 215, 304, 500.

Civil, Military, and Ecclesiastical

SMITH, ARTHUR (d. 1655). Served in Pequot War.
Mason's *Narrative.*

SMITH, HENRY (REV.) (d. 1648). Commissioner appointed by Mass. to govern Conn., Mar. 1636. Minister at Wethersfield, 1637–1648.
Hazard's State Papers I. 321.

SMITH, HENRY (d. 1682?). Granted 80 acres for service in Pequot War, May 1671. (Residence, Mass.?)
Conn. Col. II. 149.

SMITH, JOHN (d. 1680). Dep. Judge (New London), Apr. 1660, May 1660; Judge (same), May 1663.
Conn. Col. I. 347, 352, 402.

SMITH, RICHARD (d. 1692). Judge (Wickford), May 1671; President, Court of Judges, Narragansett Country, May 1673, May 1674.
Conn. Col. II. 157, 198, 231.

SMITH, SAMUEL (d. 1680). Served in the Pequot War; Sergeant, Wethersfield Train Band, prior to 1658. Deputy (Wethersfield) to Conn. Leg., Nov. 1637; Assistant, Conn. Col., Mar. 1638, Apr. 1638; Deputy again, Feb. 1641, Apr. 1641, Sept. 1641, Nov. 1641, Sept. 1643, Apr. 1644, Sept. 1644, Apr. 1645, Sept. 1645, Apr. 1646, May 1647, Sept. 1647, May 1648, Oct. 1648, May 1649, Sept. 1649, Sept. 1650, Sept. 1651, May 1653, Sept. 1653, Oct. 1655, May 1656; War Committee for Wethersfield, May 1653. (Removed to Hadley, Mass.)
Conn. Col. I. 11, 13, 17, 58, 64, 67, 69, 93, 103, 111, 124, 130, 138, 149, 157, 163, 167, 185, 195, 211, 224, 240, 243, 246, 278, 281, 314.

SMITH, SAMUEL. Deputy (New London) to Conn. Leg., May 1662, Oct. 1662; Dep. Judge (New London), Apr. 1660; Lieut., New London Train Band, Feb. 1657. (Removed to Virginia.)
Conn. Col. I. 292, 347, 379, 384.

SMITH, WILLIAM (d. 1669). Clerk, Wethersfield Train Band, July 1645; Deputy (Middletown) to Conn. Leg., Sept. 1652, Aug. 1653, Sept. 1653, May 1655, Oct. 1655. (Removed to Farmington.)
Conn. Col. I. 128, 235, 245, 246, 274, 278.

SPENCER, JARED (d. *c.* 1685). Called Ensign, June 1672; Ensign, Haddam Train Band, Sept. 1675; Deputy (Haddam), Oct. 1674, May 1675, Oct. 1675, May 1676, Oct. 1676, May 1677.
Conn. Col. II. 182, 236, 249, 265, 274, 286, 300, 365.

SPENCER, THOMAS (d. 1687). Sergeant, granted 60 acres for his good service in the country, May 1671 (Pequot War service). Residence, Hartford.)
Conn. Col. II. 150.

SPENCER, WILLIAM (d. 1640). Deputy (Hartford) to Conn. Leg., Apr. 1639, Aug. 1639, Sept. 1639, Jan. 1640, Apr. 1640.
Conn. Col. I. 27, 29, 34, 41, 46.

STAFFORD, THOMAS. Granted 50 acres, Oct. 1674. (Residence, Stonington?)
Conn. Col. II. 238.

STAIRES, THOMAS (d. 1640). Sergeant in Pequot War.
Mason's *Narrative*. Conn. Col. I. 17.

STANDISH, THOMAS (d. 1693). Granted 50 acres, Oct. 1671 (for Pequot War service). (Residence, Wethersfield.)
Conn. Col. II. 161.

STANLEY, JOHN (d. 1706). Served in Pequot War. Deputy (Farmington) to Conn. Leg., May 1659, May 1664, Oct. 1664, May 1665, Oct. 1665, May 1666, Oct. 1666, May 1667, Oct. 1667, May 1668, May 1669, Oct. 1669, May 1670, May 1671, Oct. 1671, Oct. 1673, May 1674, Oct. 1676; Ensign, Farmington Train Band, Oct. 1674; Lieut., Hartford County Troop, Aug. 1675; Lieut., King Philip's War, Sept. 1675; Lieut., Hartford County Troop, Oct. 1675; Capt., Hartford County Troop, Jan. and June 1676.
Conn. Col. I. 334, 425, 431. II. 14, 24, 31, 46, 58, 70, 82, 105, 116, 127, 147, 159, 209, 221, 230, 238, 267, 286, 347, 364, 400, 458. Shepard.

STANLEY, NATHANIEL (d. 1712). Ensign, Hartford Train Band, May 1675; Ensign, Hartford County Troop, Aug. 1675.
Conn. Col. II. 252, 347.

STANTON, JOHN (d. 1713). To join Army with 10 men of his County, Feb. 1676.
Conn. Col. II. 409.

STANTON, THOMAS, SR. (d. 1677). Served in the Pequot War. Indian Interpreter (Marshal), Conn. Col., Apr. 1638 (dismissed Apr. 1646), Jan. 1649; Deputy (Hartford) to Conn. Leg., May 1651; Deputy (Stonington), May 1666, Oct. 1666, May 1667, Oct. 1667, May 1668, Oct. 1668, May 1669, Oct. 1669, May 1670, Oct. 1670, May 1671, Oct. 1671, May 1672, Oct. 1672, May 1673, Oct. 1673, May 1674; Judge (Stonington), Oct. 1664 to 1677 incl. Indian Commissioner and Overseer, May 1666; Indian Committee, May 1668, May 1671; Commissioner to Ninigret (Niantic Sachem), May 1672; Commissioner to R. I., May 1668, Oct. 1668. Granted 250 acres, Oct. 1667.
Conn. Col. I. 19, 139, 175, 218, 435. II. 17, 31, 32, 37, 39, 47, 63, 70, 77, 82, 83, 84, 88, 89, 94, 103, 105, 106, 116, 127, 131, 136, 147, 152, 157, 159, 170, 178, 184, 192, 209, 221, 250, 275, 304.

CIVIL, MILITARY, AND ECCLESIASTICAL 51

STAPLES, THOMAS (d. *c.* 1688). Deputy (Fairfield) to Conn. Leg., Sept. 1649, Sept. 1650, Oct. 1661.
Conn. Col. I. 195, 211, 372.

STARK, AARON (d. 1685). Granted 50 acres, Oct. 1670 (for Pequot War service). (Residence, Mystic.)
Conn. Col. II. 144.

STEBBING, EDWARD (d. 1668). Deputy (Hartford) to Conn. Leg., Apr. 1639, Apr. 1640, Feb. 1641, Apr. 1641, Sept. 1641, Nov. 1641, May 1648, May 1649, Sept. 1649, May 1650, Sept. 1650, May 1651, Sept. 1651, May 1652, July 1653, Sept. 1653, Sept. 1654, May 1655, Oct. 1655, May 1656, Oct. 1656.
Conn. Col. I. 27, 46, 58, 64, 67, 69, 163, 185, 195, 207, 211, 218, 224, 231, 245, 246, 264, 274, 278, 281, 282.

STEDMAN, JOHN (d. 1675). Sergeant, to accompany Capt. Pynchon from Springfield to Fort Albany, July 1666; Lieut., Hartford Train Band, Oct. 1673; Scout, King Philip's War, Feb. 1676.
Conn. Col. II. 43, 210, 390, 408.

STEELE, JAMES. Granted 150 acres, Oct. 1672. Commissary, King Philip's War, Aug. 1675.
Conn. Col. II. 187, 358, 483.

STEELE, JOHN (d. 1665). Commissioner appointed by Mass. to govern Conn., Mar. 1636; Assistant, Conn. Col., Apr. 1636, Sept. 1636, Mar. 1637, May 1637; Deputy (Hartford) to Conn. Leg., Mar. 1638, Apr. 1638, Apr. 1639, Sept. 1639, Jan. 1640, Apr. 1640, Feb. 1641, Apr. 1641, Sept. 1641, Nov. 1641, Apr. 1642, Aug. 1642, Mar. 1643, Apr. 1643, Sept. 1643, Apr. 1644, Sept. 1644, Apr. 1645, Sept. 1645, Dec. 1645; Deputy (Farmington), Apr. 1646, Oct. 1646, May 1647, Sept. 1647, Sept. 1648, Jan. 1649, May 1649, Sept. 1649, May 1650, Sept. 1650, May 1651, May 1652, Sept. 1652, May 1653, Sept. 1653, May 1654, Sept. 1654, May 1655, Oct. 1655, May 1656, Oct. 1656, Feb. 1657, May 1657, Oct. 1657, May 1658, Oct. 1658; War Committee for Farmington, May 1653, Oct. 1654.
Hazard's State Papers I. 321. Conn. Col. I. 1, 3, 8, 9, 13, 17, 27, 34, 41, 46, 58, 64, 67, 69, 71, 73, 82, 84, 93, 103, 111, 124, 130, 133, 138, 145, 149, 157, 166, 174, 185, 195, 207, 211, 218, 231, 235, 240, 243, 246, 256, 263, 264, 274, 278, 280, 282, 288, 297, 306, 315, 323.

STEELE, JOHN, JR. (d. 1653). Ensign, Farmington Train Band, Oct. 1651.
Conn. Col. I. 227.

STEELE, SAMUEL (d. 1685). Deputy (Farmington), May 1669, Oct. 1669, May 1670, Oct. 1670, May 1671, Oct. 1671, May 1672, Oct. 1672, May 1673, Oct. 1674, May 1675, Oct. 1675, May 1676, May

1677; called Ensign, 1669; Lieut., Farmington Train Band, Oct. 1674. Granted 200 acres, May 1672.
> Conn. Col. II. 105, 116, 127, 136, 147, 159, 169, 174, 184, 192, 235, 238, 249, 265, 274, 300.

STEVENS, THOMAS (d. 1685). Corporal, N. H. Col. Troop, June 1654. (Residence, Guilford.) Deputy (Killingworth), May 1671.
> N. H. Col. II. 109. Conn. Col. II. 147.

STICKLAND, JOHN (d. *c.* 1672–3). Served in the Pequot War; Deputy (Fairfield) to Conn. Leg., Sept. 1641; first called Sergeant, Nov. 1636. (Removed to Jamaica.)
> Conn. Col. I. 6, 67.

STILES, THOMAS (d. after 1673). Served in Pequot War. (Of Windsor; removed to Flushing.)
> Mason's *Narrative*.

STOCKING, SAMUEL (d. 1697). Deputy (Middletown) to Conn. Leg., May 1658, May 1659, Oct. 1659, May 1665, Oct. 1665, May 1669, Oct. 1669, Oct. 1674, Oct. 1677; Sergeant, Middletown Train Band, May 1677.
> Conn. Col. I. 315, 334, 340. II. 14, 24, 105, 116, 236, 304, 318.

STONE, JOHN (d. 1687). Granted 100 acres, Oct. 1668 (for Pequot War service). (Residence, Guilford.)
> Conn. Col. II. 100.

STONE, SAMUEL (REV.) (d. 1663). Minister at Hartford, 1635–1663. His widow and son received grant, Oct. 1663, for his service in Pequot War and since; Commissioner to treat with New Haven Colony, Oct. 1662.
> Conn. Col. I. 388, 413.

STONE, SAMUEL, JR. (REV.) (d. 1683). Minister at Wethersfield, 1667–1677.

STOUGHTON, THOMAS (d. 1661). Lieut., Windsor Train Band (promoted from Ensign), Apr. 1640; Deputy (Windsor) to Conn. Leg., Apr. 1639, Aug. 1639, Jan. 1640, Apr. 1640, Apr. 1643, Sept. 1643, Dec. 1645, Oct. 1646, May 1647, Sept. 1647, May 1648.
> Conn. Col. I. 27, 29, 41, 46, 48, 84, 93, 133, 145, 149, 157, 163.

STOW, SAMUEL (REV.) (d. 1704). Harvard College, 1645. Minister at Middletown, 1653 ff.; at Simsbury, 1681–1685.

STREAM, JOHN (d. 1685). Confirmed Ensign, Milford Train Band, July 1665; Ensign of same, May 1669.
> Conn. Col. II. 21, 107.

STREET, NICHOLAS (REV.) (d. 1674). Minister at Taunton, Mass., 1637–1659; at New Haven, 1659–1674.

STREET, SAMUEL (REV.) (d. 1717). Harvard College, 1664. Minister at Wallingford, 1673-1710.

STRICKLAND, see STICKLAND.

SWAYNE, DANIEL (d. 1691). Deputy (Branford), May 1673, Oct. 1673, May 1674, Oct. 1674, May 1675, Oct. 1676, Oct. 1677.
Conn. Col. II. 192, 209, 221, 236, 249, 286, 318.

SWAYNE, SAMUEL (d. before 1692). Lieut. (chief military officer), Branford Train Band, Mar. 1654; Deputy (Branford) to N. H. Leg., May 1653, May 1655, May 1656, May 1657, May 1658, May 1659, May 1661, May 1662, May 1663, Oct. 1663, Jan. 1664, May 1664; Deputy (Branford) to Conn. Leg., Apr. 1665, May 1665, Oct. 1665; Judge (Branford), May 1654, May 1655, May 1656, May 1657, May 1665. (Removed to Newark, N. J.)
N. H. Col. II. 2, 52, 96, 141, 148, 169, 172, 214, 215, 232, 298, 403, 451, 488, 500, 513, 544. Conn. Col. I. 439. II. 13, 18, 24.

SWAYNE, WILLIAM (d. *c.* 1658). Commissioner appointed by Mass. to govern Conn., Mar. 1636; Assistant, Conn. Col., Sept. 1636, Mar. 1637, May 1637, Nov. 1637; Deputy (Wethersfield) to Conn. Leg., Sept. 1641, Nov. 1641, Apr. 1642, Aug. 1642, Mar. 1643; Assistant, Conn. Col., Apr. 1643, Apr. 1644; Judge (Branford), May 1654, May 1655, May 1656, May 1657.
Hazard's State Papers I. 321. Conn. Col. I. 3, 8, 9, 11, 67, 69, 71, 73, 82, 84, 103. N. H. Col. II. 96, 148, 172, 215.

TAINTOR, CHARLES (d. 1658). Deputy (Fairfield) to Conn. Leg., May 1647, May 1648.
Conn. Col. I. 149, 163.

TAINTOR, MICHAEL. Deputy (Branford), May 1670, May 1672.
Conn. Col. II. 127, 169.

TALCOTT, JOHN (d. 1660). Deputy (Hartford) to Conn. Leg., May 1637, Mar. 1638, Apr. 1638, Aug. 1639, Sept. 1639, Jan. 1640, Apr. 1640, Feb. 1641, Apr. 1641, Sept. 1641, Nov. 1641, Apr. 1642, Aug. 1642, Mar. 1643, Apr. 1643, Sept. 1643, Apr. 1644, Sept. 1644, Apr. 1645, Sept. 1645, Dec. 1645, Apr. 1646, Oct. 1646, May 1647, Sept. 1647, May 1648, Sept. 1648, May 1649, Sept. 1649, May 1650, Sept. 1650, May 1651, Sept. 1651, May 1652, Sept. 1652, May 1653, Sept. 1653; Treasurer, Conn. Col., May 1652, May 1654, May 1655, May 1656, May 1659; Assistant, Conn. Col., May 1654, May 1655, May 1656, May 1657, May 1658, May 1659; Commissioner for United Colonies, May 1656, May 1657, May 1658.
Conn. Col. I. 9, 13, 17, 29, 34, 41, 46, 58, 64, 67, 69, 71, 73, 82, 84, 93, 103, 111, 124, 130, 133, 138, 145, 149, 157, 163, 166, 185, 195, 207, 211, 218, 224, 231, 235, 240, 246, 256, 274, 280, 281, 297, 299, 314, 315, 334.

LIST OF OFFICIALS

TALCOTT, JOHN, JR. (d. 1688). Ensign, Hartford Train Band, June 1650; first called Captain, Oct. 1660. Deputy (Hartford) to Conn. Leg., May 1660, Oct. 1660, June 1661, Oct. 1661; Assistant, Conn. Col., May 1662 to 1677 incl.; Treasurer, Conn. Col., May 1660 to 1675 incl. (declined 1676 and 1677); Patentee, Royal Charter, 1662; Commissioner for United Colonies, 1663, 1669, 1671, 1673, 1676; Commissioner to treat with N. H. Col., Mar. 1663; Commissioner on N. Y. Boundary, Oct. 1663; Commissioner on Mass. and R. I. Boundaries, Oct. 1664; Committee for Indian Controversy, May 1671; Committee on Indian Complaints, May 1674; Committee on Indians, Oct. 1676; Militia Committee, July 1666; Commissioner, R. I. Boundary, May 1672; Chief Military Officer, Hartford County, June 1672; Major, Hartford County, Aug. 1673; Commander-in-Chief, vs. N. Y., Nov. 1673; member of War Council, Nov. 1673, July 1675, May 1676; Commander-in-Chief, May 1676.

Conn. Col. I. 210, 347, 353, 365, 369, 372, 378, 384, 396, 399, 410, 425, 435. II. 4, 13, 30, 44, 57, 58, 82, 104, 105, 108, 122, 126, 146, 154, 157, 169, 173, 183, 191, 192, 206, 218, 219, 221, 225, 248, 261, 274, 275, 279, 280, 284, 287, 300.

TALCOTT, SAMUEL (d. 1691). Judge (Wethersfield), 1669, 1670, 1671, 1672, 1673, 1674, 1675, 1676, 1677; Deputy (Wethersfield), Oct. 1669, May 1670, Oct. 1670, May 1671, May 1672, Oct. 1672, May 1673, Oct. 1673, May 1674, Oct. 1674, May 1675, May 1676, Oct. 1676, May 1677, Oct. 1677; member of War Council, Oct. 1675, May 1676; Lieut., Wethersfield Train Band, May 1677. Granted 200 acres, Oct. 1669.

Conn. Col. II. 106, 115, 123, 127, 130, 136, 147, 152, 169, 170, 183, 192, 209, 221, 235, 248, 249, 270, 274, 275, 284, 286, 300, 304, 305, 318.

TAPP, EDMUND (d. 1654). Assistant, N. H. Col., Oct. 1643. (Residence, Milford.)

N. H. Col. I. 112.

THEALE, JOSEPH. Deputy (Stamford), Oct. 1671, Oct. 1673, Oct. 1674, May 1675, Oct. 1675, Oct. 1676, Oct. 1677.

Conn. Col. II. 160, 209, 236, 249, 265, 286, 318.

THOMPSON, THOMAS (d. 1655). Deputy (Farmington) to Conn. Leg., May 1650.

Conn. Col. I. 207.

THORNTON, THOMAS. Deputy (Stratford) to Conn. Leg., May 1651; War Committee for Stratford, May 1653.

Conn. Col. I. 218, 243.

THRALL, WILLIAM (d. 1679). Granted 50 acres for service in Pequot War, May 1671. (Residence, Windsor.)

Conn. Col. II. 150.

Civil, Military, and Ecclesiastical 55

TIBBALS, THOMAS (d. 1703). Sergeant, N. H. Col. Troop, June 1654; confirmed Sergeant, Milford Train Band, July 1665. Granted 50 acres for service in Pequot War, May 1671.
N. H. Col. II. 108. Conn. Col. II. 21, 147.

TIBBITTS, HENRY (d. 1713). Constable (Wickford), Oct. 1670.
Conn. Col. II. 138.

TINKER, JOHN (d. 1662). Deputy (New London) to Conn. Leg., May 1660, Oct. 1660; Judge (New London), Apr. 1660, May 1660, May 1661.
Conn. Col. I. 347, 352, 354, 365.

TITHARTON, DANIEL (d. 1661). Deputy (Stratford) to Conn. Leg., May 1647, May 1649, May 1652, May 1654.
Conn. Col. I. 149, 185, 231, 256.

TOPPING, THOMAS (d. 1688). Deputy (Wethersfield) to Conn. Leg., Aug. 1639, Sept. 1639; Assistant, Conn. Col., May 1651, May 1652, May 1653, May 1655, May 1656, May 1659, May 1660, May 1661, Oct. 1662, May 1663, May 1664, 1674 to 1677 incl.; Patentee, Royal Charter, 1662 (name erroneously stated as John); Judge (Southold), Oct. 1663; first called Captain, May 1655; Capt., New Haven County Troop, May 1673; member of War Council, Nov. 1673, July 1675, May 1676.
Conn. Col. I. 29, 34, 218, 231, 240, 274, 280, 334, 347, 364, 384, 399, 414, 425. II. 4, 199, 219, 221, 248, 261, 274, 284, 300.

TRACY, THOMAS (d. 1685). Served in the Pequot War; first called Ensign, Oct. 1664. Deputy (Norwich) to Conn. Leg., Oct. 1662, May 1663, Oct. 1663, May 1667, Oct. 1667, May 1670, Oct. 1670, May 1672, May 1673, Oct. 1673, May 1675, May 1676, Oct. 1676, May 1677, Oct. 1677; Lieut., New London County Troop, Aug. 1673; Muster Master, New London County, Nov. 1673; Quartermaster, July 1675, June 1676; Committee on Stonington Indians, Oct. 1666. Granted 400 acres, Oct. 1667.
Conn. Col. I. 384, 399, 410, 432. II. 56, 59, 70, 74, 126, 136, 170, 192, 206, 209, 218, 249, 274, 286, 300, 318, 332, 455.

TREAT, JAMES (d. 1709). Deputy (Wethersfield), May 1672, May 1673, Oct. 1673, May 1674.
Conn. Col. II. 169, 192, 209, 221.

TREAT, RICHARD (d. 1670). Deputy (Wethersfield) to Conn. Leg., Apr. 1644, Sept. 1644, Apr. 1645, Sept. 1645, Dec. 1645, Apr. 1646, Oct. 1646, May 1647, Sept. 1647, May 1648, Sept. 1648, May 1649, Sept. 1649, May 1650, Oct. 1650, May 1651, Sept. 1651, May 1652, Sept. 1652, May 1653, Sept. 1653, May 1654, Sept. 1654, May 1655, Oct. 1655, May 1656, Feb. 1657, May 1657, Oct. 1657; Assistant,

Conn. Col., May 1658, May 1659, May 1660, May 1661, May 1662, Oct. 1662, May 1663, May 1664; Patentee, Royal Charter, 1662; Ensign, Wethersfield Train Band, Feb. 1653; Corporal, Conn. Col. Troop, Mar. 1658.

    Conn. Col. I. 103, 111, 124, 130, 133, 138, 145, 149, 157, 163, 166, 185, 195, 207, 212, 218, 224, 231, 235, 237, 240, 246, 256, 264, 274, 278, 281, 288, 297, 306, 309, 314, 334, 347, 365, 378, 384, 398, 425. II. 4.

TREAT, ROBERT (d. 1710). Deputy (Milford) to N. H. Leg., May 1653, May 1654, May 1655, May 1656, May 1658; Assistant, N. H. Col., May 1659, May 1660, May 1661, May 1662, May 1663, May 1664 (declined); Assistant (provisional appointment, Conn. Col.), Oct. 1664; Deputy (Milford) to Conn. Leg., Oct. 1665. Lieut. (chief military officer), Milford Train Band, May 1654; Captain of same, May 1661, confirmed July 1665; Assistant, 1673, 1674, 1675; Dep. Governor, 1676, 1677; Second Military Officer, New Haven County, June 1672; Capt., New Haven County Troop, Aug. 1673; Major, New Haven County, Aug. 1673; Second Commander, vs. N. Y., Nov. 1673; member of War Council, Nov. 1673, July 1675, May 1676; Commander-in-Chief, Aug. 1675, confirmed Oct. 1675; Committee on Indian Complaints, May 1674. Granted 300 acres, May 1673.

    N. H. Col. II. 2, 92, 99, 141, 169, 231, 297, 359, 402, 410, 451, 488, 542, 543. Conn. Col. I. 437. II. 21, 23, 183, 191, 200, 206, 218, 219, 221, 225, 248, 261, 266, 273, 284, 300, 354, 383.

TROWBRIDGE, THOMAS (d. 1702). Commissary, vs. N. Y., Nov. 1673; Lieut., New Haven County Troop, May 1675.

    Conn. Col. II. 218, 256.

TRY, MICHAEL (d. 1677). Deputy (Fairfield) to Conn. Leg., Oct. 1657.

    Conn. Col. I. 306.

TURNER, NATHANIEL (d. 1647). Captain (chief military officer), New Haven Train Band, Sept. 1640; Judge (New Haven), Oct. 1639, Oct. 1640; Deputy (New Haven) to N. H. Leg., Oct. 1643, Mar. 1644, Oct. 1644, Mar. 1645, Oct. 1645.

    N. H. Col. I. 21, 40, 44, 111, 125, 129, 147, 156, 171.

TUTHILL, JOHN. Judge (Southold), Apr. 1642. (Returned to England.)

    N. H. Col. I. 70.

UNDERHILL, JOHN (d. 1672). Served in the Pequot War; Deputy (Stamford) to N. H. Leg., Apr. 1643; Dep. Judge (Stamford), Apr. 1643; called Captain.

    N. H. Col. I. 85.

CIVIL, MILITARY, AND ECCLESIASTICAL 57

USHER, ROBERT (d. 1669). Deputy (Stamford) to Conn. Leg., May 1665, May 1667; Judge (Stamford), Oct. 1662, May 1663.
Conn. Col. I. 389, 405. II. 14, 59.

VENTRUS, WILLIAM (d. 1701). Sergeant, Haddam Train Band, Sept. 1675.
Conn. Col. II. 365.

VOWLES, see FOWLES.

WADSWORTH, JOHN (d. 1689). Deputy (Farmington), May 1672, Oct. 1672, May 1673, Oct. 1673, May 1674, Oct. 1674, May 1675, Oct. 1675, May 1676, Oct. 1676, Oct. 1677; Judge (Farmington), 1676, 1677; called Sergeant, 1672; Ensign, Hartford County Troop, Aug. 1673; Muster Master, Hartford County, Nov. 1673; member of War Council, Nov. 1673, July 1675, May 1676. Granted 200 acres, May 1672.
Conn. Col. II. 169, 174, 184, 192, 206, 209, 218, 219, 221, 235, 249, 261, 265, 274, 275, 284, 286, 304, 318.

WADSWORTH, JOSEPH (d. 1730). Sergeant, King Philip's War, Sept. 1675; Lieut., Hartford County Troop, Jan. 1676, Feb. 1676.
Conn. Col. II. 363, 400, 411.

WADSWORTH, WILLIAM (d. 1675). Collector (Hartford), Feb. 1638. Deputy (Hartford) to Conn. Leg., Sept. 1652, Oct. 1656, Feb. 1657, Aug. 1657, Oct. 1657, May 1658, Oct. 1658, May 1659, Oct. 1659, May 1660, Oct. 1660, May 1661, May 1662, Oct. 1662, May 1663, Oct. 1663, May 1664, Oct. 1664, May 1665, Oct. 1665, May 1666, Oct. 1666, May 1667, Oct. 1667, May 1668, Oct. 1668, May 1669, Oct. 1669, May 1670, Oct. 1670, May 1671, Oct. 1671, May 1672, Oct. 1672, May 1673, Oct. 1673, May 1674, Oct. 1674, May 1675; Committee on Stonington and Indian bounds, May 1666; Indian Commissioner, May 1666; Militia Committee, July 1666; War Committee, Aug. 1673; Committee on Indian Complaints, May 1674. Granted 300 acres, Oct. 1669.
Conn. Col. I. 12, 235, 282, 288, 300, 306, 315, 323, 334, 340, 347, 353, 365, 378, 384, 399, 409, 425, 431. II. 13, 23, 31, 33, 37, 44, 46, 58, 69, 82, 93, 105, 115, 123, 126, 136, 147, 159, 169, 183, 192, 204, 209, 221, 225, 235, 248.

WAKELEE, HENRY (d. 1690). Granted 50 acres, May 1669 (for Pequot War service). (Residence, Stratford.)
Conn. Col. II. 112.

WAKEMAN, JOHN (d. 1661). Judge (New Haven), Oct. 1641, Apr. 1642, Oct. 1642, Apr. 1643, Oct. 1643, Mar. 1644, Oct. 1644, May 1655, May 1656, May 1657, May 1658, May 1659, May 1660; Deputy (New Haven) to N. H. Leg., Apr. 1646, Oct. 1646, Oct. 1647, May 1648, May 1655, May 1656, May 1657, May 1658, May 1660;

LIST OF OFFICIALS

Treasurer, N. H. Col., May 1655, May 1656, May 1657, May 1658, May 1659, May 1660; Assistant, N. H. Col., May 1661 (declined).
N. H. Col. I. 58, 69, 78, 85, 119, 125, 148, 227, 274, 354, 381. II. 140, 141, 168, 169, 213, 231, 297, 359, 402. N. H. Town I. 240, 277, 313, 353, 402, 453.

WAKEMAN, SAMUEL (d. 1641). Constable (Hartford), Apr. 1636.
Conn. Col. I. 1.

WAKEMAN, SAMUEL (REV.) (d. 1692). Minister at Fairfield, 1665–1692. Granted 200 acres, May 1673.
Conn. Col. II. 200.

WALKER, ZECHARIAH (d. 1700). Minister at Jamaica, L. I., 1663–1668; at Stratford, 1668–1670; at Woodbury, 1670–1700.

WALLER, WILLIAM. (d. 1672–74.) Ensign, Saybrook Train Band, Oct. 1661; Deputy (Saybrook) to Conn. Leg., Oct. 1663, Oct. 1664, May 1665; Deputy (Lyme), May 1668, Oct. 1668, May 1669, May 1671, Oct. 1671, May 1672; Lieut., Lyme Train Band, Oct. 1671.
Conn. Col. I. 375, 410, 431. II. 14, 83, 94, 106, 147, 159, 166, 170.

WARD, ANDREW (d. 1659). Commissioner appointed by Mass. to govern Conn., Mar. 1636; Collector (Wethersfield), Feb. 1638; Assistant, Conn. Col., Apr. 1636, Sept. 1636, Mar. 1637, May 1637; Deputy (Wethersfield) to Conn. Leg., Nov. 1637, Mar. 1638, Apr. 1638, Aug. 1639, Sept. 1639, Jan. 1640; Judge (Stamford), Oct. 1642; Dep. Judge, Apr. 1643; Deputy (Stamford) to N. H. Leg., Apr. 1644; Assistant, N. H. Col., Oct. 1646; Deputy (Fairfield) to Conn. Leg., May 1648, May 1649, Sept. 1649, May 1650, Sept. 1650, May 1651, May 1652, May 1653, Sept. 1653,* May 1654, Sept. 1654, May 1655, May 1656, Oct. 1658; War Committee for Fairfield, May 1653, Oct. 1654.
Hazard's State Papers I. 321. Conn. Col. I. 1, 3, 8, 9, 11, 12, 13, 17, 29, 34, 41, 163, 185, 195, 207, 211, 218, 231, 240, 243, 246, 256, 264, 274, 281, 323. N. H. Col. I. 78, 85, 129, 275.
*Name printed as Andrew *Winard* in this entry.

WARD, JOHN. Deputy (Branford), May 1666.
Conn. Col. II. 31.

WARD, LAWRENCE. Deputy (Branford) to N. H. Leg., May 1654, May 1658, May 1659, May 1661, May 1662, May 1663, Oct. 1663, Jan. 1664, May 1664; Deputy (Branford) to Conn. Leg., May 1665, Oct. 1666; Judge (Branford), May 1654, May 1655, May 1656, May 1657, May 1665, 1666. (Removed to Newark, N. J.)
N. H. Col. II. 92, 96, 148, 172, 215, 232, 298, 403, 451, 488, 500, 513, 544. Conn. Col. II. 13, 18, 32, 46.

WARD, NATHANIEL (d. 1664). Deputy (Hartford) to Conn. Leg., May 1656, Oct. 1656. (Removed to Hadley, Mass.)
Conn. Col. I. 281, 282.

CIVIL, MILITARY, AND ECCLESIASTICAL 59

WARD, WILLIAM (d. 1676). Sergeant, Surgeon in King Philip's War, Jan. and May 1676.
Conn. Col. II. 286, 400.

WARHAM, JOHN (REV.) (d. 1670). Minister at Dorchester, Mass., 1630-1636; at Windsor, 1636-1670.

WARNER, JOHN (d. 1679). Granted 50 acres, Oct. 1671 (for Pequot War service). (Residence, Farmington.)
Conn. Col. II. 161.

WARNER, ROBERT (d. 1690). Deputy (Middletown) to Conn. Leg., May 1660, Oct. 1660, May 1661, Oct. 1661, Oct. 1662, May 1663, May 1664, Oct. 1665.
Conn. Col. I. 347, 354, 365, 372, 384, 399, 425. II. 24.

WATERBURY, JOHN (d. 1658). Judge (Stamford), May 1657, May 1658.
N. H. Col. II. 215, 235.

WATTS, THOMAS (d. 1683). Ensign, Hartford Train Band, Oct. 1673; Lieut. of same, May 1675; Capt., Hartford County Troop, Oct. 1675; fourth in command of Army, King Philip's War, Nov. 1675; Capt., Hartford County Troop, Jan. 1676, Feb. 1676, Sept. 1677.
Conn. Col. II. 210, 251, 267, 386, 388 (name misprinted as Wells), 400, 411, 506.

WEBB, RICHARD (d. 1665). Deputy (Norwalk) to Conn. Leg., May 1655.
Conn. Col. I. 274.

WEBSTER, JOHN (d. 1661). Deputy (Hartford) to Conn. Leg., May 1637, Mar. 1638, Apr. 1638; Assistant, Conn. Col., Apr. 1639, Apr. 1640, Apr. 1641, Apr. 1642, Apr. 1643, Apr. 1644, Apr. 1645, Apr. 1646, May 1647, May 1648, May 1649, May 1650, May 1651, May 1652, May 1653, May 1654, May 1657, May 1658, May 1659; Dep. Governor, Conn. Col., May 1655; Governor, Conn. Col., May 1656; Commissioner for United Colonies, May 1654; War Committee for Hartford, May 1653, Oct. 1654.
Conn. Col. I. 9, 13, 17, 27, 46, 64, 71, 84, 103, 124, 137, 149, 163, 185, 207, 218, 231, 240, 243, 256, 257, 263, 273, 280, 297, 314, 334.

WEBSTER, ROBERT (d. 1676). Deputy (Middletown) to Conn. Leg., Sept. 1653, May 1654, Sept. 1654, May 1655, Mar. 1656, May 1656, Oct. 1656, Feb. 1657, Oct. 1657, Aug. 1658, Oct. 1658, May 1659; Lieut., Middletown Train Band, May 1654; War Committee for Middletown, Oct. 1654. Granted 300 acres, May 1672.
Conn. Col. I. 246, 256, 258, 264, 274, 279, 281, 283, 288, 306, 318, 323, 334. II. 171.

WELCH, THOMAS (d.1681). Deputy (Milford) to N. H. Leg., May 1654, May 1655, May 1657, May 1658, May 1659, May 1661, May

1662, May 1663, Oct. 1663, Jan. 1664, May 1664; Deputy (Milford) to Conn. Leg., May 1665, May 1669; Judge (Milford), May 1665.
N. H. Col. II. 92, 141, 213, 231, 297, 403, 451, 488, 500, 513, 544. Conn. Col. II. 13, 17, 105.

WELLS, HUGH (d. 1678). Drummer, Conn. Col. Troop, May 1653; Ensign, Wethersfield Train Band, May 1677.
Conn. Col. I. 243. II. 305.

WELLES, JOHN (d. 1659). Deputy (Stratford) to Conn. Leg., May 1656, Oct. 1656, May 1657, Oct. 1657; Assistant, Conn. Col., May 1658, May 1659.
Conn. Col. I. 281, 283, 297, 306, 314, 334.

WELLES, SAMUEL (d. 1675). Deputy (Wethersfield) to Conn. Leg., Oct. 1657, May 1658, Oct. 1658, May 1659, Oct. 1659, May 1660, May 1661, Oct. 1661, May 1675; Judge (Wethersfield), May 1665 to 1675 incl.; Ensign, Wethersfield Train Band, Mar. 1658; Lieut. of same, May 1665; Capt., May 1670; member of War Council, July 1675.
Conn. Col. I. 306, 311, 315, 323, 334, 340, 347, 365, 372. II. 14, 17, 32, 63, 84, 106, 130, 132, 152, 170, 192, 221, 248, 249, 261. His name on page 388 is a misprint for Watts.

WELLES, THOMAS (d. 1660). Assistant, Conn. Col., Mar. 1637, May 1637, Nov. 1637, Feb. 1638, Mar. 1638, Apr. 1638, Apr. 1639, Apr. 1640, Apr. 1641, Apr. 1642, Apr. 1643, Apr. 1644, Apr. 1645, Apr. 1646, May 1647, May 1648, May 1649, May 1650, May 1651, May 1652; Treasurer, Conn. Col., Apr. 1639, May 1648, May 1649, May 1650; Secretary, Conn. Col., Apr. 1641, Apr. 1643, Apr. 1644, Apr. 1645, May 1647; Commissioner for United Colonies, May 1649, May 1654, May 1659; Moderator (in absence of Dep. Gov., the Gov. being dead), Mar. 1654; Dep. Governor, Conn. Col., May 1654, May 1656, May 1657, May 1659; Governor, Conn. Col., May 1655, May 1658; War Committee for Wethersfield, May 1653, Oct. 1654.
Conn. Col. I. 8, 9, 11, 13, 17, 27, 46, 64, 71, 84, 103, 124, 137, 149, 163, 185, 187, 207, 218, 231, 243, 251, 256, 257, 264, 273, 280, 297, 314, 334.

WELLES, THOMAS, JR. (d. 1668). Quartermaster, Conn. Col. Troop, Mar. 1658; Patentee, Royal Charter, 1662; Deputy (Hartford) to Conn. Leg., May 1662; Assistant, 1668.
Conn. Col. I. 309, 378. II. 4, 82.

WELLS, WILLIAM (d. 1671). Deputy (Southold) to N. H. Leg., June 1653, May 1659; Judge (Southold), May 1657, May 1659, May 1661, May 1662.
N. H. Col. II. 4, 215, 298, 304, 406, 456.

WESTWOOD, WILLIAM (d. 1661). Commissioner appointed by Mass. to govern Conn., Mar. 1636; Assistant, Conn. Col., Apr. 1636,

CIVIL, MILITARY, AND ECCLESIASTICAL 61

Sept. 1636; Deputy (Hartford) to Conn. Leg., Apr. 1642, Aug. 1642, Mar. 1643, Apr. 1643, Sept. 1643, Apr. 1644, Sept. 1644, Apr. 1646, Oct. 1646, Sept. 1647, May 1648, Sept. 1648, Sept. 1651, May 1652, Sept. 1652, May 1653, Sept. 1653, May 1654, Sept. 1654, May 1655, Oct. 1655, May 1656; War Committee for Hartford, May 1653.
Hazard's State Papers I. 321. Conn. Col. I. 1, 3, 71, 73, 82, 84, 93, 103, 111, 138, 145, 157, 163, 166, 224, 231, 235, 240, 243, 246, 256, 264, 274, 278, 281.

WETHERELL, DANIEL (d. 1719). Judge (New London), 1667, 1668, 1669, 1670, 1671, 1672, 1675, 1676, 1677; Deputy (New London), May 1669, Oct. 1669, Oct. 1670, May 1671, May 1675, Oct. 1676, May 1677; Commissary for Army, May 1676. Granted 100 acres, May 1675.
Conn. Col. II. 63, 84, 106, 116, 131, 136, 147, 152, 170, 249, 250, 254, 275, 287, 300, 304, 442.

WHEELER, JOHN (d. 1690). Deputy (Fairfield) to Conn. Leg., Oct. 1657, May 1658, May 1659, May 1660, Oct. 1671, May 1672, Oct. 1672, Oct. 1674, May 1677. Granted 100 acres, May 1672.
Conn. Col. I. 306, 315, 334, 347. II. 159, 170, 178, 183, 235, 300.

WHEELER, THOMAS (d. 1676). Ensign, Conn. Col. Troop, May 1653, having previously held title of Lieut. (Residence, Fairfield, Stratfield, Derby; returned to Concord, Mass.)
Conn. Col. I. 243.

WHEELER, THOMAS (d. 1673). Deputy (Milford), May 1670, Oct. 1670, May 1671.
Conn. Col. II. 127, 136, 147.

WHEELER, THOMAS (d. 1685). Deputy (Stonington), Oct. 1673.
Conn. Col. II. 209.

WHITE, NATHANIEL (d. 1711). Deputy (Middletown) to Conn. Leg., Oct. 1659, May 1661, Oct. 1661, May 1662, Oct. 1662, May 1663, Oct. 1663, May 1664, May 1665, May 1666, Oct. 1666, May 1667, May 1668, Oct. 1668, May 1669, Oct. 1669, May 1670, Oct. 1670, May 1671, Oct. 1671, May 1672, May 1673, May 1674, Oct. 1674, May 1675, Oct. 1675, May 1676, Oct. 1676, May 1677, Oct. 1677; Judge (Middletown), 1669, 1670, (Middletown and Haddam), 1672, 1673, 1674, 1675, 1676, 1677; called Ensign, May 1668; Lieut., Middletown Train Band, May 1677.
Conn. Col. I. 340, 365, 372, 379, 384, 399, 410, 425. II. 14, 31, 47, 58, 82, 94, 105, 106, 116, 126, 131, 136, 147, 159, 170, 192, 221, 236, 249, 250, 265, 274, 275, 287, 300, 304, 318.

WHITEHEAD, SAMUEL (d. 1690). Corporal, New Haven Train Band, Aug. 1642; Sergeant of same, June 1652, confirmed July 1665 (resigned June 1673); Sergeant, N. H. Col. Troop, June 1654. Granted 50 acres for service in Pequot War, May 1671.
N. H. Col. I. 76. II. 108. N. H. Town I. 131. II. 311. Conn. Col. II. 23, 150.

WHITFIELD, HENRY (REV.) (d. 1657). Minister at Guilford, 1639–1650. (Returned to England.)

WHITING, JOHN (REV.) (d. 1689). Harvard College, 1657. Minister at Hartford, 1660–1670; Second Church, Hartford, 1670–1689. Chaplain, King Philip's War, Aug. 1675. Granted 200 acres, Oct. 1672.
Conn. Col. II. 187, 355.

WHITING, WILLIAM (d. 1647). Deputy (Hartford) to Conn. Leg., May 1637, Nov. 1637; Assistant, Conn. Col., Apr. 1641, Apr. 1642, Apr. 1643, Apr. 1644, Apr. 1645, Apr. 1646, May 1647; Treasurer, Conn. Col., Apr. 1641, Apr. 1643, Apr. 1644, Apr. 1645, May 1647; Commissioner for United Colonies, Jan. 1647.
Conn. Col. I. 9, 11, 64, 71, 84, 103, 124, 137, 147, 149.

WHITMAN, ZACHARY (d. 1666). Deputy (Milford) to N. H. Leg., Apr. 1644.
N. H. Col. I. 129.

WHITMORE, JOHN (d. 1656). Deputy (Stamford) to N. H. Leg., Oct. 1643.
N. H. Col. I. 112.

WHITMORE, THOMAS (d. 1681). Deputy (Middletown) to Conn. Leg., Sept. 1654; War Committee for Middletown, Oct. 1654.
Conn. Col. I. 264.

WILCOXSON, WILLIAM (d. 1652). Deputy (Stratford) to Conn. Leg., May 1647.
Conn. Col. I. 149.

WILFORD, JOHN (d. 1678). Deputy (Branford), Apr. 1665, Oct. 1665, May 1666, Oct. 1666, May 1667, Oct. 1667, Oct. 1668, May 1669, Oct. 1669, May 1671, Oct. 1671, Oct. 1672, May 1673, Oct. 1673, May 1674, Oct. 1674, May 1675, Oct. 1675, May 1676, Oct. 1676, May 1677; Judge (Branford), 1665 to 1677 incl.
Conn. Col. I. 439. II. 18, 24, 31, 32, 46, 59, 63, 70, 84, 94, 106, 116, 131, 147, 152, 160, 170, 184, 192, 193, 209, 221, 236, 249, 250, 265, 274, 276, 286, 300, 304.

WILKINS, WILLIAM. Judge (Gravesend), May 1664.
Conn. Col. I. 429.

WILLARD, JOSIAH (d. 1674). Granted 100 acres, Oct. 1669, and 50 acres more, Oct. 1671. (Residence, Wethersfield.)
Conn. Col. II. 124, 161.

WILLIAMS, ROGER. Deputy (Windsor) to Conn. Leg., May 1637. (Removed to Dorchester, Mass.)
Conn. Col. I. 9.

WILLIS, see WYLLYS.

CIVIL, MILITARY, AND ECCLESIASTICAL 63

WILSON, ANTHONY (d. 1662). Deputy (Fairfield) to Conn. Leg., Apr. 1646.
Conn. Col. I. 138.

WILTON, DAVID (d. 1678). Deputy (Windsor) to Conn. Leg., Apr. 1646, May 1650, Sept. 1650, May 1651, Sept. 1651, May 1652, Sept. 1652, May 1653, Sept. 1653, May 1654, Oct. 1655. First called Ensign, Mar. 1658; War Committee for Windsor, May 1653. (Removed to Northampton.)
Conn. Col. I. 138, 207, 211, 218, 224, 231, 235, 240, 243, 246, 256, 278, 309.

WINARD, ANDREW, see ANDREW WARD.

WINCHELL, DAVID (d. 1723). To accompany Capt. Pynchon from Springfield to Fort Albany, July 1666.
Conn. Col. II. 43. (Residence, Windsor; removed to Suffield.)

WINES, BARNABAS. Corporal, Southold Train Band, prior to May 1654; Deputy (Southold) to Conn. Leg., May 1664.
N. H. Col. II. 97. Conn. Col. I. 425.

WINSTON, JOHN (d. 1697). Corporal, New Haven Train Band, Mar. 1661; Sergeant of same, Aug. 1665.
N. H. Town I. 474. II. 145.

WINTHROP, FITZJOHN (d. 1707). Deputy for New London, Oct. 1671; Commissioner to R. I., Oct. 1668, May 1670, Oct. 1670, May 1671, May 1672; called Capt., Oct. 1668; Chief Military Officer, New London County, June 1672. (Removed to Boston.)
Conn. Col. II. 103, 131, 146, 156, 173, 183.

WINTHROP, JOHN (d. 1676). Assistant, Conn. Col., May 1651, May 1652, May 1653, May 1654, May 1655, May 1656; Governor, Conn. Col., May 1657, May 1659 to 1675 incl.; Dep. Governor, Conn. Col., May 1658; Colonial Agent to King, June 1661; Patentee, Royal Charter, 1662; Commissioner for United Colonies, May 1658 to 1666 incl., 1669; Militia Committee, July 1666; member of War Council, Nov. 1674, July 1675; Agent to England, July 1675.
Conn. Col. I. 218, 231, 240, 256, 274, 280, 297, 314, 315, 334, 347, 348, 364, 365, 369, 378, 379, 384, 398, 399, 425, 430. II. 4, 13, 18, 30, 39, 44, 57, 82, 104, 108, 126, 146, 169, 191, 219, 220, 248, 261, 263.

WINTHROP, WAITSTILL (d. 1717). Capt., New London Train Band, May 1665. Commissioner to R. I., Oct. 1668; Commander of New London County forces, July 1675; Commissioner for United Colonies, Oct. 1675.
Conn. Col. II. 14, 103, 271, 332.

WISE, JOHN (REV.) (d. 1725). Harvard College, 1673; preached in Branford, 1675. Chaplain, King Philip's War, Jan. 1676. (Became minister at Chebacco in Ipswich, Mass.)
Conn. Col. II. 399.

WOLCOTT, HENRY (d. 1655). Constable (Windsor), Apr. 1636; Collector (Windsor), Feb. 1638. Deputy (Windsor) to Conn. Leg., Apr. 1639; Assistant, Conn. Col., Apr. 1643, Apr. 1644, Apr. 1645, Apr. 1646, May 1647, May 1648, May 1649, May 1650, May 1651, May 1652, May 1653, May 1654, May 1655; War Committee for Windsor, May 1653.
Conn. Col. I. 1, 12, 27, 84, 103, 124, 137, 149, 163, 185, 207, 218, 231, 240, 243, 256, 274.

WOLCOTT, HENRY, JR. (d. 1680). Deputy (Windsor) to Conn. Leg., Oct. 1655, Oct. 1660, May 1661; Assistant, Conn. Col., May 1662 to 1677 incl.; Patentee, Royal Charter, 1662; Militia Committee, July 1666; member of War Council, Nov. 1673, July 1675, May 1676. Granted 300 acres, Oct. 1669.
Conn. Col. I. 278, 353, 365, 378, 384, 399, 425. II. 4, 13, 30, 44, 57, 82, 104, 123, 126, 146, 169, 191, 219, 248, 261, 274, 284, 300.

WOLCOTT, SIMON (d. 1687). Deputy (Simsbury), Oct. 1671, May 1673, May 1675; First Officer, Simsbury Train Band, Aug. 1673.
Conn. Col. II. 159, 192, 208, 209, 249.

WOOD, JOHN (d. 1637). Killed in Pequot War.
Conn. Col. I. 29.

WOOD, JONAS (d. 1689). Judge (Huntington), May 1663, May 1664.
Conn. Col. I. 401, 428.

WOODBRIDGE, BENJAMIN (REV.) (d. 1710). Minister at Windsor Second Church, 1668–1681. (Returned to Mass.)

WOODBRIDGE, JOHN (REV.) (d. 1691). Granted 250 acres for a farm, Oct. 1671. Minister at Killingworth, 1666–1679; at Wethersfield, 1679–1691.
Conn. Col. II. 163.

WOOSTER, EDWARD (d. 1689). Constable (Derby), Oct. 1669.
Conn. Col. II. 118.

WOODHULL, RICHARD (d. 1690). Judge (Setauket), May 1661, May 1664; Deputy (Setauket) to Conn. Leg., May 1664.
Conn. Col. I. 366, 425, 428.

WYATT, JOHN. Ensign, Hartford County Troop, Feb. 1676, June 1676, Sept. 1677.
Conn. Col. II. 411, 458, 506.

WYLLYS, GEORGE (d. 1645). Assistant, Conn. Col., Apr. 1639, Apr. 1640, Apr. 1643, Apr. 1644; Dep. Governor, Conn. Col., Apr. 1641; Governor, Conn. Col., Apr. 1642.
Conn. Col. I. 27, 46, 64, 71, 84, 103.

Civil, Military, and Ecclesiastical

WYLLYS, SAMUEL (d. 1709). Assistant, May 1654 to 1677 incl.; Patentee, Royal Charter, 1662; Moderator, 1670, 1671; Commissioner for United Colonies, 1662, 1666, 1667, Oct. 1669, 1671; Commissioner to treat with N. H. Col., Oct. 1662, Mar. 1663, Aug. 1663; Commissioner for Mass. and R. I. Boundaries, Oct. 1664; Militia Committee, July 1666; Committee on Indians, May 1668; Commissioner to R. I., Oct. 1670, May 1671, May 1672; member of War Council, Nov. 1673, July 1675, May 1676; Agent to N. Y., Apr. 1676. Granted 100 acres, May 1668.
Conn. Col. I. 256, 274, 280, 297, 314, 334, 347, 364, 378, 379, 384, 388, 396, 398, 407, 425, 435. II. 4, 13, 30, 39, 44, 57, 68, 82, 91, 104, 126, 146, 154, 156, 169, 173, 219, 221, 248, 261, 274, 284, 300, 426.

YALE, THOMAS (d. 1683). Deputy (New Haven), May 1672.
Conn. Col. II. 169.

YOUNGS, JOHN (CAPT.) (d. 1698). Judge (Southold), May 1661, May 1662, Oct. 1662, May 1663, 1674; Deputy (Southold) to Conn. Leg., Oct. 1662; Assistant, Conn. Col., May 1664.
N. H. Col. II. 406, 457. Conn. Col. I. 386, 390, 402, 425. II. 229.